DISCOVERY

LEADER'S GUIDE

God's Answers to Our Deepest Questions

a Bible Study by Will Wyatt

Discovery: God's Answers to Our Deepest Questions
Leader's Guide
By Will Wyatt

Published by

A ministry of The Navigators, P.O. Box 6000, Colorado Springs, CO 80934

The Navigators is an international Christian organization called to advance the Gospel of Jesus and His Kingdom into the nations through spiritual generations of laborers living and discipling among the lost.

Dawson Media is a ministry of The Navigators that aims to help Navigator staff and laypeople create and experiment with new ministry tools for personal evangelism and discipleship.

Editor: Leura Jones
Designer: Steve Learned

Unless otherwise noted, all Scriptures are taken from the New American Standard Bible (NASB), ©1960, 1962, 1963, 1968, 1971, 1972, 1973, 1975, 1977.

Printed in the United States of America
ISBN: 0-9729023-1-7

TABLE OF CONTENTS

Acknowledgments

My sincere appreciation goes to Jennifer Freeman and my wife, Betty, for their valuable help in developing this Leader's Guide.

INSTRUCTIONS FOR USING THE LEADER'S GUIDE

An important question Christians should ask themselves is this: When we go to be with the Lord, what will we take with us into eternity? From Scripture, the only thing I can ascertain that we'll take with us is the depth of our trust and love relationship with the Lord that we have established here on earth. Paul makes it clear in 2 Corinthians 4:17–18 that the depth of the trust relationship developed on earth will impact our eternity in ways we can't even imagine. This should make us more serious about what we focus on in life and give us a desire to know how God says this relationship should develop.

The goal of *Discovery* is to help Christians grow in their relationship with the Lord by:
- Understanding foundational truths in the Bible
- Looking at how Scripture defines who we are and what God expects of us
- Moving knowledge we have about God from our heads to our hearts so that we can have a fuller, more intimate relationship with Him
- Embracing our total dependence on God and seeking to walk in that dependence in a daily abiding, trusting relationship

To do this, the study will cover:
- Scriptural truths about God and about us that form the basis for our relationship
- The provisions God has made to develop the relationship
- What our responsibility is in building the relationship
- How the relationship is lived out in some practical areas

My prayer is that this study will increase the reader's intimate, comfortable, and trusting love relationship with God and that he or she will *know* God, not just *know about* God.

Our heads seek information, and our hearts seek experience. This study is geared toward both. As the Lord transforms us into His image, He allows us to be put in situations in which we have to apply what we know is true. The questions in *Discovery* are designed to help people grapple with this process and to ensure that the path they are on is biblical.

Your Discipling Ministry

If you are the facilitator leading one or several others through this study, you are involved in discipling. One of the best definitions Scripture gives of discipling is found in 2 Timothy 2:2.

And the things which you have heard from me in the presence of many witnesses, these entrust to faithful [people], who will be able to teach others also.

God shares His discipling ministry with us, and it is one of the primary ways we grow our relationship with Him. We get to see God bless others, but the greatest blessing may be ours as we see Him demonstrate His grace and love. As you guide others through this study, you will probably be the one who is most blessed.

The Importance of Small Groups

In my years of experience using this study, I have found small groups to be the single most important factor in how much people are able to understand the principles and apply them to their lives. Sharing and discussing force us to clarify our thoughts so that we can verbalize them. Small groups also help many people think through things they otherwise might not.

Organizing Your Group

The ideal size of a *Discovery* discussion group is no more than eight people, plus the facilitator. If your group is significantly larger than this, divide into smaller groups and try to enlist some others who have been through the study to facilitate. Because each chapter builds on the previous one, it is advisable not to have people join the group after the second or, at most, the third chapter. Ideally everyone should start together at the beginning, because after the second or third chapter it is almost impossible to catch up.

The best environment for using *Discovery* is a group that is committed to meet together for a significant amount of time, such as during a school year. This will allow group members to adequately cover the content and work at incorporating the truths into their lives. Next best would be a commitment of 20 to 22 weeks. Twenty-two weeks allows two weeks on each chapter. With 20 weeks it is feasible to take one week each for chapters one and two, then two weeks for each of the remaining chapters. Some groups can meet for only 11 weeks, taking one chapter per week. Often these groups will choose to repeat the study later.

Regardless of your schedule, you may want to have an extra meeting or social time at the end to go over the last question on page 223: "What has God taught you from this entire study that has changed your relationship with Him?"

Because some of the questions are of a personal nature, same-sex groups work best. Occasionally married couples meet together in small group and this may be your format. If it is possible to break up into same-sex groups for at least part of the time, people will feel more freedom to share. The mixed group could then get back together to share what was important and discuss more general points.

Before You Begin

The questions at the end of each chapter are designed to help apply the principles learned in that chapter. Many questions ask for answers of a personal nature. Some groups have been meeting together for some time, know each other well, and have developed comfort and trust with one another.

If this is not true of your group, most of the participants will not be willing at first, if at all, to be honest and vulnerable, and far less will be accomplished in the group. It is extremely important to break down as many barriers as possible before you start. In our program with college students, we begin with each member telling life stories. They also spend time socializing. I highly recommend that you begin with some social functions to get to know one another. These can be dinners and/or fun activities. Make sure there is time devoted to sharing lives, and allow time for group members to ask questions. Either tell life stories or select several of the following questions, or similar ones, that would be suitable to the circumstances of your group.

The first person to begin will set the tone that others will follow. It is best if you start and share some significant things that will make others feel comfortable doing the same. Consider questions such as these:

- When you were a child, what was your favorite holiday and why?
- What is your favorite sport or hobby?
- What has been your schooling and/or career experience?
- Describe a "dream date."
- How did you meet and marry your spouse?
- How many children do you have, what are their ages, and what do they do now?
- If you could travel anywhere in the world, where would you like to go and why?
- What are some of your dreams and goals?
- Who has been the most influential person in your life?
- Share an embarrassing moment or a funny or unusual experience.
- What is/was your family like? Christian or non-Christian?
- What experiences or people have affected you positively or negatively?
- Tell your story about how you received Christ.
- What has been significant in your growth since?

Group Commitments

Your group will avoid potential problems if everyone makes and understands certain agreements. At the first meeting, have everyone in the group make the following commitments. (You could even type these up and have each member sign a copy.) Each member should agree:

- *Never to repeat anything shared in confidence outside the group.* This is extremely important and is the only way people will be comfortable enough to be honest and real.
- Except for emergencies, *to attend every meeting and to be on time.* Tell your group that you will start on time, even if all members are not there.
- *To read each chapter, write out the answers to the questions, and come to the meeting prepared to share.* Some people may want to participate in the discussions without having read the material or answering the questions. It can be very disruptive if people share (or argue) about what they "feel" or what they "think" without knowing the content of the chapter.
- *To study the chapters in order.* Because the study is so progressive, with each chapter building on the previous ones, agreeing to study the chapters in order will help keep people from jumping ahead and spending time on topics that will be covered indepth later.
- *To stay focused on the material* in the chapter and not get sidetracked with peripheral issues.

If these commitments are made before you start, then you and the other members can gently hold one another accountable.

Finally, find out at your first meeting who is comfortable praying out loud with others and who is not. Assure them that you will not call on them to pray unless they want you to.

How to Lead Your Small Group

Remember that God is the one who teaches and interprets His Word in the hearts of others. Your responsibility is to be prepared and to trust the Lord with what happens in your group. Pray before each meeting for the members of your group and for His direction as you meet.

Also remember that this is the group's meeting, not yours. The leader's only job is to facilitate the discussion, to keep it on track, and to clarify the truths presented in *Discovery* if group members have a hard time understanding them. This is not a time to teach.

The following points will help you make the most of your small group's time together:

- Do not take turns sharing the position of facilitator. The group is more likely to stay on track and not stray into side issues if the same person leads each meeting.

- It is not a good idea to do up-front teaching of the material. Doing this may cause some group members to not read the material and will reduce the amount of time you have for group discussion. Reading the chapters individually and then discussing them in the group is the most effective way to learn from *Discovery*.

- Encourage your group members to read and then reread the entire chapter, or listen to the audio tape or CD, if they have it.[1] Recommend that the group members use the study in quiet times so they have time to read or reread the chapter each week you remain on it.

- If you are covering a chapter a week, do not regularly add prayer time or other forms of worship to your meeting time. You will need as much time as possible to discuss the chapter. You will probably want to open with a short prayer asking for the Lord's guidance, but remember not to call on those who are uncomfortable praying aloud. There will be times when you sense that your group needs to share and pray together, or a situation may arise in which you need to stop and pray for an individual who is struggling or hurting. In general, however, reserve your time for discussing the study.

- Arrange the seating in a circle so that people sit comfortably close to one another and have good eye contact. Keep the setting as informal and relaxed as possible.

- If you, as the facilitator, ask the questions, the tendency will be for everyone to direct their answers to you. At your first meeting, inform people that they are sharing with the entire group, and ask them to look at and address their answers to the group, not just to you. You will probably have to remind them of this several times throughout the study.

---

1 A set of 10 (Chapter 1 and 2 are combined) audio tapes or CDs of my summer teaching is available for $25.00, including shipping. The content is similar to *Discovery*. Please see the last page of this book for information on how to order.

- If you have people who are repeating the study, on some questions they might share how they answered the first time and how their answer may be different now.

- Many of the questions involve answers of a very personal nature. Encourage your group members to share only what they are comfortable with. Also remind them that being vulnerable to share our lives with other believers often has rich rewards: close bonds of friendship, accelerated spiritual growth in our lives, and being more honest with God. As time goes on, confidence in the group will increase.

- Discipling is modeling more than teaching. Be a model to your group by being vulnerable. Share your struggles and areas in which you are hurting or don't have the answers.

- If you must cover a chapter a week, you may not get to every question. Before each meeting, choose the questions you feel are the most important and make sure you get to these. The guide to each chapter gives suggestions about important questions.

- You do not have to ask the questions in order. In fact, it sometimes helps if you occasionally vary the way you lead the group. You might want to jump to a particular question if someone brings up that subject.

- Always ask the last question in each chapter about what was most significant to them. You may even want to ask this question first. Their answers may be an important point from the chapter, or they may be minor points or statements that God made very significant and real to them.

- Use the second-to-the-last question in each chapter to help your group summarize the main points presented. The question asks, "If you were to share the information presented in this chapter with a friend, what main points would you communicate?" The points should apply to not only the facts, but also the application to our relationship with the Lord, with other people, and to our circumstances. See the answers in this guide for help.

- Do not let your group get distracted by side topics. Even from the beginning, the study may bring up questions that will be answered later. If you know the topic will be covered later (prayer, God's will, and so forth), ask the group to hold their questions until that particular topic is addressed. Other topics may come up that are not addressed in *Discovery*. Sometimes if an extra topic comes up and people start discussing it immediately, it is fine to let them interact a very short time. Then interrupt and tell them it will either be addressed later or should be set aside until after the study is finished.

- Especially in the early weeks of meeting together, members of your group may make comments that you know not to be biblically true. When you have people who will stay together through the entire study, it is not necessary to challenge them, knowing that God will reveal truth to them as the study progresses. Whenever disagreement happens, be gentle and respect people's opinions. Remind them to see what Scripture says, not merely to rely on "Well, I think . . ." or "I've heard. . . ."

- Disagreement and conflict are not always bad. Most of us have to struggle with what Scripture says, what we have learned in the past, or what other people tell us, and this struggle is often the way we learn. Everyone comes from a different spiritual background. It is important to recognize and respect each other's differences while focusing on the main things. However, don't let disagreement get out of hand in your group. If conflict or disagreement arises, pray for the Lord's leading in when to stop it with love, grace, and gentleness. Sometimes it is wise to ask people to discuss it with you or others outside of your meeting time.

Possible Group-Dynamic Problems

Following are some issues that could come up in any group situation and suggestions for how to handle them.

- *Quiet members.* Get to know your members. Some may be intimidated in group situations. Ask them privately what they are comfortable with. Let your group know that you will ask everyone what was significant to them and occasionally will ask the quiet members to answer other questions. As comfort increases in the group, the quiet ones will probably answer more readily.
- *Overly talkative members.* Some people cannot stand a period of silence or just naturally dominate conversations. Talk to them one-on-one and ask them to help you draw out others by waiting to answer or asking others what they think.
- *Superficial sharing.* Set the example by sharing significant and personal things about yourself. When a member gives a superficial answer, ask them specific questions to draw out deeper answers. You may also need to talk to them on the side.
- *Argumentative or "always right" members.* Avoid arguing the points. State the ground rules of respect but remind the group of the commitment to stay focused and not get off on side issues. Remind the group that the focus of the study is our growing, trusting relationship with the Lord, things we can all agree on.
- *Monopolizing the group with personal problems.* Talk to the member individually, explaining the problem. Remind them of the group's focus. If you're comfortable, ask them to talk to you alone about their personal crisis, or suggest they get help from other sources.
- *Rarely prepared members.* Privately remind the members of their commitment to read the chapter and write out the answers. Ask if this is something they can follow through with or if they need to participate in a group later when they have the time to prepare.

Don't Get Sidetracked

In addition to the topics covered in the study, your group may bring up questions about other doctrinal issues. Do not get sidetracked by other issues. This is why one of the commitments is to stay focused on the material at hand. If your group stays together and the issues remain important, you could choose to study these other topics and how they relate to our personal relationship with the Lord after finishing *Discovery*.

Common questions people have that are not addressed in this study involve end times, gifts of the Spirit, predestination, and election. These are areas on which believers can agree to disagree, and these topics should be set aside. This Leader's Guide will warn you of issues and questions that may be encountered in each chapter.

The most common doctrinal issues that will arise in this study involve predestination and election. It is important to stay focused on the primary purpose of the study, which is not how we got into God's family, but how we walk with Him now in this new relationship. Most of the questions about election, free will, and predestination center on how we were reestablished into our relationship with God. There can be honest disagreement about this area of theology, and there are some questions that we may not fully understand until we are in heaven. God does not give us full explanation of some of His sovereign ways. Still, we do not have the right to disregard or avoid what He says in Scripture out of our lack of understanding or discomfort. Encourage your group that if they study this topic later, to always go to Scripture and ask God to be their teacher.

Using This Guide

At the beginning of each chapter in the Leader's Guide is a primary goal for the *Discovery* chapter, an overview, the points that are important to clearly understand before moving on, and any possible issues that might come up with suggestions about how to handle them.

The guide then gives a brief explanation of what the questions are designed to do, followed by each question in *Discovery* and some answers that you will probably get from your group. Do not read the answers to your group. Use the comments here merely as your guide to make sure the question or subject is adequately covered before you move on. The answers will also give you some ideas to suggest if the group is having a hard time answering or participating. Not everything listed in the guide needs to be covered.

I cannot emphasize enough the importance of encouraging everyone to write out the answers. Those who write out the answers will be most able to grasp and internalize the material. They will get more than twice as much out of it. They will also come much more prepared for discussion and sharing. You will be reminded in the first couple of chapters to encourage your group to do this.

I'm Available

I pray that you will be blessed in a special way as you go through this study and as you share with your group what God is doing in your life. Please contact me if I can be of help or if you have questions that are not clearly answered. I would like to hear how God is teaching you.

Will Wyatt
Discipleship Focus
223 Young Life Lane
Branson, MO 65616
(417) 338-8804
wyatt@dfocus.org

For information about Discipleship Focus, our summer-long discipleship program for college and career-age young adults, please go to www.dfocus.org.

Please Note: The questions in this Leader's Guide correspond to the questions in the latest edition of *Discovery*. If you have an earlier version, you may find some questions have changed slightly.

Chapter 1

WHAT KIND OF RELATIONSHIP DOES GOD WANT WITH ME?

Reminder: If you haven't already done so, please start your first meeting by having your group agree to the "Group Commitments" listed on page VII.

Please insist, as much as possible, that everyone in your group writes out their answers. You might even make it a requirement. This is key to help them grasp and internalize the truths of this study. Writing out the answers helps people carefully think through what they really believe and feel. They will also come much more prepared for discussion and sharing. Also encourage your group to share as deeply as possible. *If some people in your group are repeating the study, they may want to share how they first answered the question as well as how they answer it now.* It can be very encouraging to see how God is changing them and bringing maturity into their life.

Make sure your group members also read the Introduction to *Discovery*. If they have not, please ask them to do so.

Primary Goal of Chapter 1

To cause people to evaluate what they do, to be honest about their feelings, and to be open to comparing their Christian lifestyle with Scripture.

Overview

Our Christian life can easily become a "career" or duty, based on what we do rather than our daily, intimate, personal relationship with a loving God.

The results of this can be:
- Serious questions about the reality of the Christian life.
- Lack of joy, freedom, and a comfortable relationship with God, leaving only a legalistic burden.
- Pressure and guilt. When we haven't been taught the biblical essentials of the Christian life, we tend to live by the world's standards and modeling for our lives rather than God's. We compare ourselves with others, and that comparison often leads to guilt and ultimately burnout. Guilt, or trying to prove ourselves, is what drives us to act in ways contrary to God's plan for us.

Why does this happen?
- Lack of a scriptural basis for a healthy relationship with God. We copy what other Christians do or listen to what they tell us without verifying it with God's Word.
- Relying on feelings and experiences in our Christian lives without validating them with Scripture.

What God wants:
- Faith—a trusting and believing relationship with Him.
- To move what we know about God (head knowledge) to a place where it affects every aspect of our lives (heart knowledge).
- For us to mature by trusting God more quickly and with more situations than we have in the past.

This chapter helps us understand that we should evaluate our Christian walk not on how much we do or accomplish, but on how quickly we give our struggles to God. The goal is not for more "self-sufficiency" but for "God dependency."

Points to Emphasize

It is absolutely crucial that we personally know what *Scripture* says about our relationship with God and not just take the word of others. It is then important to let God move this knowledge from our heads to our hearts through everyday experiences. Only then will it affect every aspect of our lives and result in a growing, trusting relationship with the Lord.

Possible Issues

Usually there are none, but occasionally someone will express frustration and anger over the pressures put on them to perform. Others may not want to give up the feeling of significance they receive from all their Christian activities.

Whether or not people share easily in this chapter will depend on the size of the group and how comfortable they are with each other. That is why starting off with life stories can be so helpful. Although many of the questions are personal, most people are not hesitant to answer. If sharing does not happen easily, you can set the tone by sharing your answers. You could also suggest they share more generalized answers—things they know to be true of many Christians. If your group is still having trouble, you might say, "You may have come up with some of these things . . ." and then share a few of the answers from this Leader's Guide. That should help your group begin to open up. Do whatever you can to make everyone more comfortable.

Discussion Questions and Possible Answers

All of the questions in this chapter involve personal answers. They are designed to help people acknowledge and give voice to the guilt they feel about what they "do" and "do not do" as a Christian and to help them be honest about the masks they put up for the Christian community. The questions should help your group members realize that the Christian life is not about "doing," but about who they are becoming in Christ and the intimate relationship He wants with us. Questions 1, 3, and 7 are especially important to address.

1. What things do you do or not do that, as a Christian, produce feelings of guilt?

   Personal answers.

   This could include how much they pray, read the Word, have quiet times, or attend church. It might be their frequency or effectiveness in witnessing, the amount of time given to ministry, or tithing habits. For some it could be the way they treat members of their family, their thought life, anger, rebelliousness, how they handle temptation, or relationships with the opposite sex.

2. Give examples of situations in which you, as a Christian, feel pressure to "act" in certain ways or to "do" certain things. In each instance, try to determine if the pressure is the result of: a) expectations of other people, b) expectations you have of yourself, c) family influence or formative years, or d) other. Be specific.

   These will be personal answers.

   Some churches, pastors, youth leaders, or others who strongly influence our lives immediately stress Christian "behavior" and service—not only how we should act but what we should "do" for Christ. Sometimes parental expectations have influenced us, and occasionally we put these pressures on ourselves from what we see or hear from other Christians. Our culture and peers put great emphasis on what we do and what we produce. Draw out different examples of these pressures.

3. a) When and why do you sometimes wear a "mask"?

   Personal answers.

Sometimes we display a completely different attitude or personality trait than what we are actually feeling. Help your group members share what circumstances prompt them to wear a particular mask.

b) What feelings, attitudes, or circumstances are you trying to hide?

Personal answers.

Some people wear masks to cover up insecurities or to get certain results or reactions. Things we try to hide are marriage problems, anger and abusive conduct within homes, an appearance of peace when in reality there is anxiety, fear, and turmoil. Another mask would be attendance and participation at church and Christian functions without including Christ in everyday life. Some Christians use phrases like "praise the Lord," "if God wills," "God bless you," and others that may not be genuine but are said for the sake of appearances. We are often too scared or embarrassed, too proud, or too afraid of change to admit weakness and show our true selves.

c) In what ways do you try to cover these up?

Personal answers.

People may use humor, shyness, boisterousness, sarcasm, friendliness, and other styles of relating to cover up their inner feelings.

4. Christian maturing is trusting the Lord 1) more quickly and 2) with more situations. What things do you currently have trouble trusting God with?

Personal answers.

Tell your group members that at the end of this study they will want to refer back to their answers to see if their ability to trust the Lord has increased.

5. To what degree do you experience joy, peace, and a sense of God's love?

Personal answers.

6. If you were to share the information presented in this chapter with a friend, what main points would you communicate?

(This question will appear in every chapter. It is not necessary to touch on all the answers given in this Leader's Guide. These are merely suggestions of answers you may get from your group.)

Your group might include in their answers some of these points:

a) Many of the questions, problems, and struggles with guilt in our Christian lives come from failure after trying to do things *for* Christ before we know exactly what He expects us to do and how we are to do them.

b) The importance of knowing fundamental biblical principles.

c) The importance of personally verifying from Scripture what others say the Bible teaches.

d) The importance of moving things from our heads to our hearts, which usually occurs through life experiences and circumstances—either difficult ones or comfortable ones.

e) Maturing is a process. It is a progressively shorter elapsed time between trying to handle situations on our own and turning them over to God.

f) Although trusting may sometimes result in visible changes or accomplishments, what is important to God is *how much* we trust Him, not what we accomplish.

7. From your journal page or highlighted text, what points—major or minor—were most significant to you and why?

Personal answers.

Writing out this answer is important to help us review and organize our thoughts.

DO I MATTER
TO GOD?

Reminder: Please tell your group again of the importance of writing out the answers.

Primary Goal of Chapter 2

To help Christians realize how much God loves them, that He is constantly available to them, and that He continually cares for them.

Overview

We have to start living by the understanding on page 10 of *Discovery*: 1) The truest thing about God is what He says about Himself, not what we think He is like; 2) the truest thing about us is what God says about us, whether or not we believe it or "feel" it to be true.

We usually view ourselves based on our circumstances and the opinions of people important to us. Our feelings of significance are often a result of our appearance, possessions, intelligence, education, profession, success, or other worldly things.

God views each of us as significant as any other believer. He desires a relationship with us that is more intimate than we can imagine.

- God knows everything about us, the good and the bad. He knows what we think, what we are going to say, what gives us joy, and what makes us sad (Psalm 139).
- His hand of blessing is always on our head and He is working for our good, even in our struggles and what may seem like tragedies in our lives. (We will talk more about this later when we address God's purpose for believers in Chapter 4.)
- God made each of us unique individuals. He "knew" us before we were formed in the womb.
- God thinks about us constantly.

- God wants us to realize that we, as His adopted children, are as important to Him as Jesus Christ. We can also get to know Him as well as Moses, David, Mary, or any other believer who has ever lived. He wants us to respond to His incredible love.

Points to Emphasize

The truest thing about us is what God says about us, not what we think about ourselves. He created each of us individually, thinks about us constantly, and loves us unconditionally.

Possible Issues

For many of us, because of past experiences and a lack of human models who love us unconditionally, the truth that God loves us as much as He does may be difficult to believe. It will only become real to us as God moves it from our heads to our hearts through a process of life experiences.

Please Note: Please inform your group that the remaining chapters are longer, have more questions, and will take more time to prepare.

Discussion Questions and Possible Answers

The questions in this chapter again involve personal answers. They are designed to make us see where we gain our significance and begin to realize how much God really loves us. Depending on their life circumstances, it may take time for many to even believe this as fact (head knowledge) and even longer for it to become heart knowledge in a way they *know* it to be true. Questions 1, 2, 3, 5, and 7 are especially important to address.

1. Psalm 139 and the verses on the next pages tell us how significant we are to God.

   a) Do you struggle with lack of self-confidence or poor self-image? In what areas or under what circumstances?

   Personal answers.

   Most everyone experiences a lack of confidence in certain situations. A surprising number of people feel very inadequate most of the time. Encourage your group to share.

   b) Why do you think you experience this?

   Personal answers.

   The world places such importance on money, education, success, material possessions, talents, leadership abilities, positions, and appearance. Unfortunately, this is even true in many Christian groups. Ask if (and why) it helps to know that the importance of the people in Hebrews 11 was their trust in God rather than their accomplishments. Trusting God and including Him in our lives is something we all can do.

2. In what ways, or from whom, do you try to gain a feeling of significance?

   Personal answers.

   Some people try to gain a feeling of significance from their education, their job or profession, their appearance, their money and material possessions, or their success and position in the community. Some use sports or other talents as a way to feel significant. Christians may try to gain significance through serving people in ministry or church. Many people try to gain a sense of significance from other people. They may try to know and be friends with powerful or respected people. Many people feel significant only with those they are close to: spouses, boyfriends or girlfriends, parents, close friends, or family.

3. It's clear from Psalm 139 that God created each of us just the way we are: our appearance and personality; our interests, abilities, and talents; our intelligence; and what family we were born into. Are there things about you or your family circumstances that you wish were different?

   Personal answers.

   Many of us compare ourselves to others and feel that we come up short. It is sometimes hard to trust that God made us the way we are for our eternal good. Many people also come from very dysfunctional or abusive families and may struggle with why God allowed this. *These issues will be addressed later in the study, so please do not let your group spend time now trying to come up with reasons for their circumstances.*

4. Read the selected portions of Psalm 139 on the next page. What has special meaning to you?

   Personal answers.

5. The truest thing about us is what God says about us, whether or not we "feel" it to be true. If you are not certain God loves you, why do you feel this way? What can you do to *experience* how much Scripture says God loves you?

   Personal answers.

   Some people have never felt truly loved by their parents or other people close to them. Some have felt inadequate as they compare themselves with siblings or peers. Others think that sin in their lives, before or after receiving Christ, makes it impossible for God to love them. These things have affected their ability to feel loved by God.

   Spending time in Scripture that talks about God's love, grace, and forgiveness will confirm what God says is true and will give them, at the least, "head knowledge" of His love for them. They should pray consistently for God to move this truth from head to heart so that they have a firm confidence of God's love and "feel" it to be true.

6. If you were to share the information presented in this chapter with a friend, what main points would you communicate?

Reminder: The answers below are merely suggestions of what your group may share. Not all of these need to be covered.

a) The truest thing about us is what God says about us, not what we feel about ourselves.

b) We are infinitely significant to God. He knew us before we were even born.

c) He created each of us a unique individual. There are no mistakes in who we are and what our circumstances are.

d) He knows *everything* about us and still loves us.

e) He is always with us, thinks about us constantly, and is always blessing us.

7. From your journal page or highlighted text, what points—major or minor—were most significant to you and why?

Personal answers.

IS GOD REALLY IN CONTROL?

Primary Goal of Chapter 3

To give a scriptural basis to the fact that a loving, sovereign God is over all and above all and that He can exercise His control at any time He chooses to accomplish His purposes. This knowledge should help us learn to trust Him more.

Overview

One of the reasons we have difficulty developing an intimate, trusting relationship with the Lord is because we don't have a biblical understanding of who He is. This chapter is designed to help us understand God's nature, particularly His sovereignty. Studying what God says about Himself, not just relying on our feelings, opinions, or experiences, will help us trust His sovereignty.

A simple definition of sovereignty is the supreme, unencumbered rulership of God. In other words, God has no equal. He is alone in His power, His wisdom, and His freedom. He is above all and is totally independent.

In this chapter, we'll look at three key aspects of God's sovereignty: 1) God does what He does because of who He is; 2) God is sovereign in His power, His knowledge/wisdom, and His freedom; and 3) His sovereignty is filtered through His goodness.

1. God does what He does because of who He is.
   - It is essential to understand that *God has no needs*. This allows Him to love unconditionally because He needs nothing in return.
   - God is so incomprehensible to the human mind that we can know nothing about Him except what He chooses to reveal to us. He has primarily revealed Himself in the Bible and through Jesus Christ. We have the responsibility to ask Him to make this revelation understandable to our minds and hearts.

2. The three aspects of God's sovereignty are:
   - His *power* is absolute. He merely spoke and the heavens and earth were formed as a demonstration of His power. Yet He bared His arm to bring us salvation.
   - His *knowledge and wisdom*. He knows and understands all things. He formed each of us in the womb and knows everything about us. This brings comfort because He knows and understands what we are going through.
   - He has total *freedom* to choose when and how He uses His power and authority.
     - God is sovereign *in individual lives*. He brought us into existence, and we are never on our own. No one will ever thwart His good purpose for us.
     - God is sovereign *in world events*. Even if things happen in the world that we do not understand, they are not out of God's control, and He permits them. They will fit into His ultimate purpose for humankind.

3. God's power, knowledge, and freedom are filtered through His *goodness*.
   - God is good and can do nothing but good. But God wants a good for us that is far greater than just meeting our material, physical, and emotional needs. God's good includes everything He causes or allows to happen so that He can conform us to His likeness (Romans 8:29).
   - Because some of the things we experience do not always seem "good" to us, we must learn to trust that God knows what is best, that He is in control of all things, and that He loves us unconditionally.

Points to Emphasize

God is sovereign and has the power, the wisdom, and the freedom to act in any way He chooses. He has ultimate and total control over everything (1 Chronicles 29:11) because He is the one who creates and maintains all life. His sovereignty, however, is always filtered through His goodness. He can do nothing but good.

Possible Issues

People who have experienced very difficult things in life may struggle with why God allowed them to happen. Others will struggle with why God allows evil in the world. Later in the study we will address some of these questions. There may be a few in your group who misconstrue the fact that God is in control of everything to mean that we are like puppets and that God dictates our every move. We will later study the areas in which God has allowed Christians free will and areas that are completely under His control.

Discussion Questions and Possible Answers

The questions in this chapter will challenge your group to compare their "ideas" of God to what Scripture says He is like (1, 2, 5a). Questions 3, 4, 5b, 5c, 7, and 8 should help people address whether they *really* believe God's sovereignty can affect their lives. Question 5a is a fill-in-the-blank question. In the few instances these types of questions appear in the study, they are designed to help key concepts stand out and be remembered.

In Question 6 we look at what *God* says our "good" is versus what we *think* is good. This subject will be developed more in the next chapter. Question 7 should be an encouragement to many. If we *understand* and *believe* (head knowledge) that God is using everything to conform us to the likeness of Jesus Christ—even those things that we don't like or understand—then it will help us *trust* Him and *experience* His love in our lives more and more (heart knowledge).

1. a)   When you picture God, what is He like?

Personal answers.

Some people think of God as a vague "force." Some think of Him as a stern policeman or disciplinarian, and others think of Him as a kind old man who overlooks everything. Others see God as someone who sets everything in motion, then sits back to see how things will work out. If people in your group are repeating this study, have them share their answers from both the first time and now.

b)   What do you think caused you to have this image?

Personal answers.

Ideas about God can come from church, Christian literature, family, peers, our relationship with our own fathers or with others in authority in our lives. These feelings can shape how we think about God.

c)   In what way has this chapter changed or strengthened your view of God?

Personal answers.

2. What illustrations of God's power were most significant to you?

Personal answers.

3. One aspect of God's sovereignty is His knowledge/wisdom.

a)   How does it make you feel that God knows and understands all your thoughts and emotions?

Personal answers.

This will be a comfort to some, possibly disconcerting to others.

b)   Do you believe that He is this involved in your life? Why or why not?

Personal answers.

4. a)   To whom do you usually go first when you have a problem or need advice? Why?

Personal answers.

Many people go to friends, parents, pastors, counselors, or other people before they think to talk to the Lord about a problem.

b) If God is not the first one you turn to, what keeps you from going to Him first?

Personal answers.

5. Freedom is also an aspect of God's sovereignty.

a) "Everything in the heavens and earth is yours, O Lord, and this is your kingdom. We adore you as being in control of ____everything!____" (1 Chronicles 29:11, TLB).

b) What situations or events has God allowed to happen in your life, or in the lives of those close to you, that are (or were) very difficult and seemed unfair?

Personal answers.

Your group's answers will probably include sickness, death of loved ones, abuse, divorce, lost jobs, lack of money, lack of close relationships, losing opportunities they thought were important, physical problems, or what they perceive as a lack in their talents, intelligence, or personality.

c) If you are angry with God because of these things or if it is hard for you to believe that He is in control or that He is good, write down how you feel. Be honest about your questions, doubts, and emotions.

Personal answers.

Assure your group members that having these questions, doubts, and feelings is OK. Encourage them to honestly express to God and to the group how they feel. Do not, at this time, try to give reasons why difficult things have happened.

6. a) What is God's definition of good for us?

God's good for us is to conform us to the image of Jesus Christ (Romans 8:28–29). He wants to produce in us the character, or likeness, of Jesus Christ.

b) How does this differ from society's idea of good?

Our society equates good with comfort, success, status, security, and lack of stress or pain.

7. a) Are there areas in your life in which you have seen God significantly change you?

Personal answers.

One of the greatest evidences we experience of God's existence is the change we have seen in our own lives.

b) In what areas would you like to see additional change?

Personal answers.

The group's level of comfort with one another will probably determine the depth of the responses. This can be a great time of sharing and encouragement.

8. Using the following list as a guide, select a few areas that are challenges in your own life right now: relationships, health, money, the future, marriage, children, difficult circumstances, ministry, fear, world events, or other areas significant to you. In each area:

a) What are your thoughts, feelings, or fears right now?

b) In what ways do you try to solve the problem or meet the need yourself, or to whom do you look for help?

c) How would believing that God is sovereign change your attitudes and responses?

These all will be personal answers.

Following are some possible answers, or you can use these to stimulate discussion. *Do not attempt to go over all these areas.* Discuss only the ones your group initiates.

Relationships—Trusting God and giving Him control of our relationships may be one of the hardest things we face. Relationship problems can produce anxiety or discouragement. They can cause us to try to manipulate circumstances, and even enlist others, to achieve the results we want. If we commit relationships to God, understanding His sovereignty helps us trust the outcome of the situation, whether or not it turns out the way we want it to.

Health—Many people have serious health problems and pain with accompanying fear and discouragement. Knowing God is in control, and that He will not allow His children any suffering that He does not also give them the grace and strength to bear, will bring more peace.

Money—We easily get caught up in securing or keeping jobs, climbing the corporate ladder, making good investments, or looking to other sources for our financial needs. We can get panicked or resentful if things don't go well or discontent if others have more than we do. Knowing about God's sovereignty should take much of the anxiety out of our attitude toward money. If God can create the universe just by speaking, and He has promised to supply our needs (Matthew 6:25–34), He surely can meet our financial needs.

Future—Psalm 139 and so much of Scripture assure us that He wants to be intimately involved in every aspect of our lives, including our future. We are often anxious about the future. We may have definite ideas of what we want to do or no idea of what we want to do. It is comforting to know that God sees around the corner, knows what is best for us, and can cause it to happen. It should help us want His plan for our lives and trust Him for it (Philippians 1:6; 1 Thessalonians 5:18).

Marriage—The fact that God loves us and has all knowledge and wisdom should help those who are in struggling marriages to respond in loving and faithful ways. They can look to God for their security and significance at times when they may not receive these assurances from their spouse.

Children—Everyone with children will tend to worry about them at times and may tend to seek advice from many sources. We can seek God's wisdom in how to raise our children and how to face all the decisions and problems that will arise. If we need to seek help from others, He can give us direction. We can trust grown children to a God who is good and is in control.

Difficult circumstances—Tough situations may evoke all kinds of emotions, from despair to anger. Sometimes we will do almost anything to get out of the situation. Knowing God is sovereign should help us have peace and trust that God knows what is best for us even when life is difficult. It should be comforting that He is in control and will only let things happen that are for our eternal good and that we can handle. He knows our limits (1 Corinthians 10:13).

Ministry—Involvement in ministry can produce pride or disappointment and discouragement. We can easily be deceived into thinking that God needs us, and this can result in distortion and abuse in ministry. It is easy to put our trust in programs, activities, our education, or our talents. Or guilt can be used to manipulate and motivate people. God's sovereignty should be tremendously significant in this area. We will study more about this later, but real ministry is done by God, not by us, even though He invites us to come be involved with Him. This should remove the pressure and guilt if the results or circumstances in ministry are not what we think they should be.

Fear—God knows what is happening to us in fearful circumstances. He controls the lives of people or situations that might harm us. This should give us peace and confidence.

World events—It may not always seem like it, but Daniel 2:21 tells us that world events are under His control. This should give us greater peace about what is happening in our governments and world events.

9. If you were to share the information presented in this chapter with a friend, what main points would you communicate?

   a) The truest thing about God is what He says about Himself, not what we think He is like.

   b) God is *sovereign* (1 Chronicles 29:11–12). He is supreme, in complete control, above all, and completely independent.

c) The three areas of God's sovereignty we looked at were:

Power—In this study the illustration was the creation of the universe. God must be able to exercise power and authority over everything and everyone to be sovereign. A secondary point was that God (Jesus Christ) merely spoke to form the universe, whereas He flexed his arm (gave of Himself) to bring us salvation.

Knowledge/wisdom—To be in control of every situation, it is necessary to have total knowledge of the situation and the wisdom to know what to do. Some illustrations given were: He knows everything about us; He *understands* all our doubts, insecurities, and fears; we should go to Him first for counsel.

Freedom—God does what He knows is best. We exist only because He chose to create us and maintain us. Men and world events are under His control because He maintains the life of every living person and can use any method He chooses to control events. He is in control of *everything*.

d) God's sovereignty is encompassed by and filtered through His *goodness*. If a sovereign God was not inherently and totally good, we would be victims subject to His whims. It is necessary to balance a study of His power, His knowledge/wisdom, and His freedom with the fact that He is good and can do nothing but good.

e) The "good" God is committed to accomplish in our lives is to conform us to His image. In other words, He shares His very existence—His very character—with us. We must be able to trust Him with our past before we will trust Him with our present and our future.

10. From your journal page or highlighted text, what points—major or minor—were most significant to you and why?

Personal answers.

DOES GOD HAVE A PURPOSE FOR MY LIFE?

Primary Goal of Chapter 4

Our Christian culture puts so much emphasis on what we do, rather than who we are in Christ, that many have formed their own ideas about God's purpose for believers. This chapter takes a biblical look at what God wants to accomplish in our lives and what He wants *us* to do.

Overview

God's purpose is to share His nature, the nature of Jesus Christ, with us.

"And we know that God causes all things to work together for good to those who love God, to those who are called according to His purpose. For whom He foreknew, He also predestined to become conformed to the image of His Son, *that He might be the first-born among many brethren"* (Romans 8:28–29, emphasis added).

In this chapter we look at:
1. *Why* God shares Himself (His likeness, His character, His very nature) with us
2. *How* He does this
3. *What* our responsibility is

1. Why God shares Himself with us
   - God does what He does because of who He is. He shares Himself with us because He loves us. He has no ulterior needs or motives.
   - God is complete within Himself and He is unchanging. Nothing that He does or does not do changes His essence. *"For I, the Lord, do not change"* (Malachi 3:6).
   - God has no needs. He created us and serves us because He chose to. *"The God who made the world and all things in it, since He is Lord of heaven and earth, does not dwell in temples made with hands; neither is He served by human hands, as though He needed anything, since He Himself gives to all life and breath and all things"* (Acts 17:24–25, emphasis added).
   - God is complete within Himself; He does not even need our praise. Our worship and praise do not add anything to who God already is. *"Blessed be Your glorious name, which is exalted above all blessing and praise!"* (Nehemiah 9:5, NKJV).
   - God cares about individuals. He knows and cares for each of us individually. He is more concerned about the relationship each of us has with Him than with a "bigger outcome" or task, as illustrated in the story of healing the woman on the way to Jairus's house.
   - God's purpose flows out of His love. God loves us so much that on the cross Jesus became sin (everything opposite to His nature) for us so that we might become righteous in Him (2 Corinthians 5:21).

   "Long ago, even before he made the world, God chose us to be his very own, through what Christ would do for us; he decided then to make us holy in his eyes, without a single fault— we who stand before him covered with his love. His unchanging plan has always been to adopt us into his own family by sending Jesus Christ to die for us. And he did this because he wanted to!" (Ephesians 1:4–5, TLB, emphasis added).

2. How does God conform us to His image?
   - God demonstrates Himself to us to give us evidence and confidence in who He is. He does this through His Word and through experiences in our daily lives.
   - He allows or brings circumstances into our lives, both positive and negative—struggles and trials, triumphs and joys—that cause us to turn to Him in ways we normally would not.
   - He allows us to be in ministry with Him, where we watch Him change and bless people's lives. Jesus never did anything on His own initiative, and neither should we. We are never to be independent contractors working for God, making our own decisions about where, when, and how to do ministry.

3. What is our responsibility in this process?
   - Our goal in life is to focus on knowing Him. *"And this is eternal life, that they may* know *Thee, the only true God, and Jesus Christ whom Thou hast sent"* (John 17:3, emphasis added).
   - How do we do this?
     - We get to know Him in His Word.
     - He reveals Himself to us in creation.
     - He shows Himself to us in answered prayer, and He intercedes in our circumstances.
     - We watch Him change the lives of others.
     - As we depend on Him to accomplish His will, He shares Himself and we know Him better.

This chapter helps us think about our daily personal relationship with God, rather than just what we know about Him. We tend to think so much about our perceived "responsibility" as a Christian that it can lead to pride and burnout. In this chapter we see that God, because of His love for us, has always intended for us to walk in relationship with Him. This relationship is characterized by intimacy, depth, and dependence on Him so that we will be in the process of being conformed to the image of Jesus Christ (Romans 8:29).

Points to Emphasize

A sovereign God has no needs. He loves us so much that Christ was willing to become sin for us. *His purpose for believers is to share Himself with us and begin the process of making us like Jesus Christ.* He wants our goal to be to get to know Him. As we do, we will be conformed to His image. His ministry—watching Him work in the lives of others—is one thing He shares with us to conform us.

Possible Issues

Some people may struggle with several truths in this chapter. It will be difficult to argue with the fact that God has no needs, but some people still believe that God created us because of His own personal need for someone to love, someone to worship Him, or someone to bring glory to Him.

Even more people may struggle because, as a motivational tool, many Christian groups teach that God needs us to serve Him in ministry to build His kingdom. Many Christians have assumed or been led to believe that the ministry of building God's kingdom was His primary purpose for them on earth. So some in your group may struggle with the fact that God's purpose for believers is to share Himself with us—which is to conform us to the image of Jesus Christ—and that He wants us to get to know Him. Ministry may be one of the vehicles He uses to accomplish both. In addition, sometimes our own significance and identity are mistakenly based on what we do in ministry or how holy our lives look.

Dependency on God can be troubling if people are looking at it for the first time, because it feels like it takes away from the significance of the task or accomplishment. That's why it's important to understand that what God wants from us is *relationship,* not *accomplishment.* Allowing us to be in ministry is not about "doing His work," but trusting Him to accomplish His purpose in us, as well as in others. (Reinforce the idea that His purpose is to transform us into the image of Christ.) This should bring freedom to people in your group. If there are those who struggle, don't force them to agree; suggest that they search Scripture and ask God to give them understanding. These truths will continue to be reinforced in later chapters.

Another possible struggle may be with the fact that the Father made Jesus, "who knew no sin to be sin on our behalf." We, in our humanness, cannot completely understand what this truly means, but all major translations state the verse in the same way. We have to believe what Scripture says—even if we cannot completely understand it. Jesus is able to give us His nature of holiness because He became our substitute and willingly took upon Himself our nature of rebelliousness (sin).

The truths and the verses we use in this chapter might bring up questions about other doctrines, although questions are more likely to come up in the next two chapters. I strongly urge you to insist that your group not spend time on these topics now. You will get bogged down with everyone's "ideas" about what is true, and it will detract from the important points in this chapter. (See the suggestions in "Don't Get Sidetracked" at the beginning of this guide.)

Discussion Questions and Possible Answers

The questions in this chapter seek to help us balance how *we* may have defined our relationship with God with how *He* defines our relationship with Him. (The truest thing about God is what He says about Himself.) Through these questions, the group will have very practical things to share about their understanding of God and how they can continue to seek to know Him in both their heads and hearts.

Questions 2 and 6a are factual questions that are crucial to know. They are the key to a biblical relationship with the Lord. Be sure that these questions are answered and understood.

Questions 4 and 5 will help your group understand the meaning of the word "glory" and why God wants to demonstrate Himself to us.

The remaining questions help internalize and apply the content of the chapter. Questions 7 and 8 deal with how ministry fits into God's purpose for us. Especially if members of your group are involved in various forms of ministry, try to spend some time on these two questions, emphasizing how we should follow Christ's example of not taking initiative.

1. a) What have you thought, or what have you heard from others, that God needs from us, or what does He depend on Christians to do for Him?

    Personal answers.

    It could be things like:
    - Our worship
    - Our love
    - To have fellowship with us
    - To have an object to love
    - To be glorified by us
    - To witness for Him
    - To bring others to Christ
    - To serve Him
    - To affect world events or governments
    - To set moral standards and atmosphere
    - To establish God's kingdom

    b) How does it make you feel to know that He has no needs?

    Personal answers.

    This will be very freeing for some; others may feel it reduces their significance.

2. a) What is God's purpose for believers? (What does He want to accomplish in our lives?)

    God wants to give us Himself (His nature), which is to conform us into the likeness of Jesus Christ. *"For whom He foreknew, He also predestined to become conformed to the image of His Son, that He might be the first-born among many brethren"* (Romans 8:29). This is the only way we can be set free from the control of sin.

    b) What, in the past, have you thought was His purpose for believers?

    Personal answers.

3. a) What specific events have occurred in your life that you feel God caused, or allowed, to accomplish His purpose?

    Personal answers.

    Many people can look back and see how God used certain circumstances or events to teach them something, to help them trust Him more, or to make them more Christlike.

    b) In what way, if any, does knowing God's purpose for you help partially answer your questions about difficult circumstances?

    When difficult circumstances come into our lives, knowing that this is often the process God uses to make us trust Him and to conform us to His likeness helps us know that things are not out of God's control. Things do not happen to us simply by chance. Knowing that God is at work in our lives, that He will not let us suffer more than what is good for us, and that He will enable us to endure takes some of the fear and questions out of difficult circumstances.

4. When God says, "whom I have created for My glory," the word "glory" means demonstration, manifestation, or revelation.

    a) What things have you done (or what have you seen others do) to try to bring glory to yourself?

    Personal answers.

    When we, as humans, speak of glory, we think of people doing things and getting recognition for them. Ask your group members to give specific examples if they can. If you do not get personal illustrations, ask them to generalize.

    b) What were your motives?

    Personal answers.

    The motive behind glory and recognition is usually pride and ego. People seek praise, recognition, and sometimes money for what they do because they want to feel important.

    c) Why does God demonstrate Himself to us, and what are His motives?

    God reveals Himself, or demonstrates Himself to us, for *our* good. It is an act of His love. He wants to share His existence and nature with us because He knows we need Him and it will be for our benefit. God does not need recognition, praise, or adoration, because He has no needs. We can give nothing to Him that will add to who He is. Instead, He serves *us* and blesses *us* by making Himself known.

5. a) What comes to your mind when Christians say, "to bring glory to God" or "to glorify God"?

It often implies that *we* should do things, say things, and live in a way that either earns God's favor or makes Him look good in the eyes of others. We are in error if we think we can add to His essence or glory. He is already as glorious as He possibly can be. The way we live should be in obedience to God, and the changes He is making in our lives are so that He can be seen in us.

b) What should this mean (2 Corinthians 4:7)?

To glorify God should mean that we give *Him* credit, thanks, and praise for everything. We recognize who He is and that *He* is already glorious and is the one who accomplishes anything good.

6. a) What goal does God want Christians to have?

The goal of our lives should be knowing God, which will result in becoming one with Him. To become one with God is the same as being conformed to His image. Our goal should be to spend time with God so that we get to know Him personally and trust Him in the situations He uses to make us more like Him.

b) What things do you do to get to know another person?

To get to know another person, we spend time with them, talk to them, listen to them, and share our own concerns and our lives with them.

c) How can you, personally, get to know God better?

Personal answers.

We should do the same with God by spending time with Him, talking to Him, and sharing all our thoughts and concerns with Him in prayer. We should listen to Him, learn about Him through Scripture, and listen to His prompting of our thoughts and desires.

7. a) What did you learn about ministry from this chapter?

Personal answers.

Real ministry—anything accomplished that has eternal significance—must be initiated by God and accomplished by Him. Even Christ said in John 5:30 (and He was especially referring to His own ministry), "I can do nothing on My own initiative." We are not to decide what we will do for God and then ask Him to bless us.

Ministry is a gift to us from God. We get to know Him better as He allows us to share in His work in the lives of others. *"Now all these things are from God, who reconciled us to Himself through Christ, and gave us the ministry of reconciliation"* (2 Corinthians 5:18).

God graciously chose to use us as His instruments of ministry to people. *God does not need to use us;* He could do it without us. But He has chosen to minister *through us* as the vehicles of *His* ministry. It is for our benefit that He allows us to be involved in His work. We are just as blessed to observe God's demonstration in ministry as the one who is being ministered to. God does not need us to help Him out, but He has chosen to include us for our benefit.

  b) Specifically, how will this affect any ministry in which you are now involved or will be in the future?

Personal answers.

Hopefully this will cause Christians to seek God's direction regarding ministry rather than initiating ministry on their own. It should cause them to trust the Lord for the results of ministry and, thereby, result in more peace. If some in your group are not involved in organized ministry, point out that these principles still apply because all of our relationships involve some form of ministry.

8. a) What was Paul's approach to ministry right after his conversion (Acts 9:19–30)?

Paul decided where, how, and to whom he would minister. He did not yet realize that God must make these decisions. He was witnessing and preaching out of his own strength. Guilt may also have motivated Paul (similar to what we discussed in the first chapter) because he had previously persecuted Christians.

  b) List any specific instances when you did the same thing in ministry or in other areas of your life such as relationships, school, jobs, or family.

Personal answers.

Encourage your group members to share if they can identify with this.

9. a) What ideas were new to you, or reinforced, regarding the events in the Garden of Gethsemane or on the cross?

Personal answers.

The idea that the Father caused Christ to be sin may be new to some. It should also help us understand how terrible sin is. Christ obviously understood and was in great anguish because He knew that by becoming sin, He would be separated from the Father. It is necessary and good for us to understand the terrible cost Christ paid because of our rebelliousness. If we really understand the horribleness of sin, then we can better understand the depth of God's love to pay such a great price for our redemption.

b) In what way, if any, does this affect your understanding and appreciation of the cross and your salvation?

Personal answers.

10. If you were to share the information presented in this chapter with a friend, what main points would you communicate?

a) God has no needs. He does what He does because of who He is. God chose to love us, and because He has no needs, He can love us unconditionally.

b) When God created us for His "glory," it means for His demonstration, revelation, or manifestation. In other words, He wants to share with us knowledge about Himself as well as sharing His character.

c) God's ultimate purpose for believers is to conform us to the image of Jesus Christ (to become one with Him).

d) The Christian's goal in life should be to know God, which will result in us becoming one with Him.

e) To conform us to His image, He uses events and circumstances that He causes or allows in our lives. We get to know Him as He continually demonstrates Himself to us, and we are progressively conformed to His image.

f) Ministry is not the purpose of our creation. It is a gift from God that enables us to know Him better as we see Him demonstrate Himself in our lives and in the lives of others. We should follow His lead in ministry; He was *always* submissive to the leading of His Father.

g) Christ *became* sin on the cross—everything opposite to His nature—so that He could give us His nature. Because of our sin, He was totally separated from and forsaken by God the Father. And He did it because He *wanted to* (Ephesians 1:4–5, TLB)!

11. From your journal page or highlighted text, what points—major or minor—were most significant to you and why?

Personal answers.

HOW DOES GOD REALLY SEE ME?

Primary Goal of Chapter 5

To help us realize how spiritually dead and separated from God we were before redemption. We also will see that we must remain totally dependent on Him because He is the only one who can control our old sin nature.

Overview

In this chapter we will examine how God sees all humans before redemption, what our position is now as His children, and how this affects the way we live and relate to God. Specifically, we'll look to Scripture to understand: 1) our human condition apart from Christ's redemption, 2) our condition and position now as followers of Christ, and 3) our limitations and responsibilities in our new relationship with Him.

1. What is the condition of all humankind apart from redemption through Jesus Christ? (In Adam)
   - Although Adam and Eve were created in the spiritual image of God, after the fall all human beings are born in the spiritual "likeness" or "image" of Adam (Genesis 5:3). Even from the womb, all people are spiritually dead, totally separated from and condemned by God, unable to hear Him, and unable to understand or do godly things. No one has ever sought God, and all are *slaves to sin*. This condition is called "the depravity of man."
   - Apart from Jesus, people constantly try to meet their basic needs of significance, security, and purpose through their own human resources. God created humankind with these needs because He wanted to meet them as an expression of His love and commitment to us. But because humans rejected the provisions that only God can meet (which was first

demonstrated by Adam and Eve), they constantly try to fill those needs themselves.

- They have Satan's nature, or the nature of rebellion. This does not mean that there is nothing but evil happening in the world, but the good that occurs is self-serving "worldly good" as opposed to "godly good," which is selfless and eternal. Satan fell from his relationship with God by seeking to be independent and free from God's authority. In fact, he wanted to be above God. Before receiving Christ, all people have the same attitude of rebellion.

2. What is our condition and position now, as followers of Christ? (In Christ)
   - God no longer condemns us, and we are no longer "slaves to sin." We are *set free from the necessity to sin* because we have the Holy Spirit (the Spirit of Christ) within us. We now can choose to depend on Christ to free us from our sin nature.
   - We no longer have to strive by our own human resources to meet our needs for significance, security, and purpose. As was His original plan in creation, God wants to meet those needs for us.
   - As we desire to have God share Himself (His nature) with us, we become less focused on ourselves and more focused on His life in us. This allows us to get to know Him better and better.

3. What are our limitations and responsibilities in our new relationship with Him? (In Christ)
   - Although we are new creations in Christ, we still struggle with the old sin nature that remains in us. God wants us to know how destructive sin was to us and that we still can be deceived into thinking we can maintain control and meet our own needs.
   - God has not restored us to the former position of Adam and Eve, who were "created" beings in a Creator/creation relationship. Instead, He has chosen to place us in His "family," children of God and joint heirs with Jesus Christ (Romans 8:17). The Father loves us as much as He does Jesus Christ, and He wants us to become "one" with Him (John 17:21–23).
   - In the process of conforming us to the likeness of Christ, God may discipline us, not because He is angry or displeased with us, but for our eternal good. The purpose is always to conform us to the likeness of Christ—to give us His character. Even in the midst of discipline, He never withholds His love or fails to give direction or meet our needs.
   - We must understand our sin condition before God redeemed us so that we can live in a healthy relationship with Him now. We came into the relationship spiritually bankrupt. We did not bring any godliness into it. Even as Christians, we have no human ability to live godly lives on our own. We must be *desperately dependent* on the Lord to do any spiritual good and to become like Christ.

Points to Emphasize

We were spiritually blind, deaf, and dead before God redeemed us. We did not bring anything godly into our relationship with Him. We must continue to be desperately dependent on Him for anything spiritual, including our Christian growth.

Possible Issues

The extent of our *total* depravity before being redeemed will come as a surprise to some people.

They may have thought we were damaged by sin but still had some good in us. This is why I have used so much Scripture in this chapter—to let God speak for Himself. Many people have found the depravity of natural man to be "freeing" because God knew our condition but still loved us and sent Jesus to bring us back to Himself.

Questions of free will and election may come up in this chapter. To avoid getting caught up in these, familiarize yourself with our suggestions on page X and XI. If your group members struggle with this chapter, don't argue with them about what they believe or how they *feel* about our sin nature. Instead, encourage them to personally study the verses and ask God to show them what they mean. Then they can determine for themselves what God is saying. Instead of getting sidetracked with how we got into God's family, focus on how we are to look to His resources to live our new lives as His children. If anyone seriously wants to find out what Scripture says about election, understanding the verses in this chapter is crucial to drawing an informed conclusion, but address these topics once the study has concluded.

Discussion Questions and Possible Answers

The questions in this chapter are designed for both "head knowledge" and "heart knowledge." Questions 2, 3, 6, and 8 deal with "head knowledge," the truth of Scripture that we *must* understand to live in right relationship with the Lord. The content of this chapter is not always clearly taught in Christian circles, but it is foundational for what will be said in the remaining chapters.

The remaining questions deal more with "heart knowledge" and should help your group personalize the truth of the chapter. Question 1 helps us realize how we may seek to meet our needs for significance, security, and purpose apart from God. Sometimes people will complain that we keep asking the same question over and over, but it's important for the group to look at the ways they strive to meet their own needs. *If they can't pinpoint this, it will be difficult for them to understand why God allows continual struggle in their lives.*

Questions 4, 5, 7, and 9 help us better understand the struggle between our old sin nature and the new life we have in Christ. It is important for your group members to feel like they can openly share their struggles with sin. This chapter teaches us that we all struggle with the sin nature, and God will use our sharing as a way to free us from the bondage of trying to live under the law. Being desperately dependent on God's provision is the only way we will ever be free from our old nature—not by trying harder or showing others how "good" we can be. When we are open to seeing ourselves honestly, God conforms us to His image. Chapter 6 will describe how we can be more dependent on Him as we learn to abide in Christ.

1. Before you became a Christian (or when you are not looking to God now):

   a) From which people or from what things did you try to gain your significance?

   Personal answers.

   It might be from parents, boyfriend/girlfriend, spouse, teacher, pastor, or other ministry leader. It may be from their athletic ability, accomplishments, or talents. People also try to gain significance from their appearance, clothes, jobs or positions, grades in school, degrees, houses, cars, and other material things.

b) To whom, or to what, did you look for material or emotional security, and in what ways?

Personal answers.

People often look to jobs or careers, bank accounts, investments, insurance, retirement funds, property, or inheritances. They may also look to spouses, unions, and government. Younger people often look to school loans, jobs, education, and parents for financial security. People of all ages may look to various relationships for emotional security.

c) What did you see as your purpose in life, and what were your goals?

Personal answers.

Secure jobs and careers, degrees, promotions, money, houses, clothes, material possessions, education, marriage, and family are all common goals. Some people have goals of making the world a better place, leaving a legacy, or gaining respect, prestige, and power.

2. What did you learn about Satan that assures you that we don't need to be afraid of him? What is our protection (see page 70)?

Personal answers.

Satan is a created being, under the complete authority of God. He is not all-present (he can't be everywhere at once), all-knowing, and all-powerful. He has no ability to harass or persecute believers unless God permits it. (Satan had to ask God permission to cause Job's trials.) Our protection is to stay close to Jesus Christ.

3. a) In whose spiritual image were Adam and Eve created (Genesis 1:26–27)?

Adam and Eve were created in God's spiritual image. It was a mirror image, not an exact likeness. They had a perfect personal relationship with God and shared His holiness and perfection.

b) In whose spiritual image was Adam's son Seth born, and all humankind since (Genesis 5:3)?

We are born in Adam's spiritual and physical image.

c) What is the difference, and why is it important to understand this?

We died spiritually, losing all aspects of God's holiness, perfection, and character in us. If we do not understand this, we may think that we still have some ability to act in godly ways and do godly things out of our own human resources.

If it comes up in your discussion, James 3:9 says that we should treat all men and women with respect because they are made in the likeness of God. The Greek word for likeness in this verse means a resemblance or similarity to God that all humans possess in that we have intelligence, emotion, and the ability to make decisions and affect our earthly environment. We no longer, however, possess any of God's holiness and goodness.

4. Jeremiah 17:9 (NKJV) says: *"The heart is deceitful above all things, and desperately wicked; who can know it?"* Suppose a non-Christian, a Christian who is not walking with God, and a Christian who is walking with God all spend the day at a local mission feeding the poor.

   a) List motives for the first two to do this.

   The motives for the non-Christian will be self-serving. It may be so that he will look good in the eyes of others, thus feeding his pride and ego. It may be done out of a sense of pressure or guilt. It may simply make him feel good about himself. The Christian not walking with God may have the same motives as the non-Christian or may be doing it because it is the "Christian thing to do." He may be serving because of peer pressure from other Christians whom he wants to impress.

   b) What motives would the Christian walking with God have?

   A Christian walking with God would be serving at the mission because he knew this was something God led him to do. He does not do it for any credit but because Christ's love for others is in control of his life. He knows that any spiritually good thing that happens is because God is at work. He is doing it because of his obedience to God's leading. He is aware that God is sharing His ministry with him, and this is how he will get to know God better and be conformed to His image, as well as serving others.

   c) List some things that non-Christians believe about "goodness" that show how deceived they are.

   Non-Christians do not even know their own heart, and they do not know how far away from God they are. Most of them are conditioned to do what society considers "good" and are totally unaware of spiritual goodness. They may compare themselves with others and conclude that they are good by that standard. They set their standards by whatever their particular society considers acceptable.

   d) How can a believer who is not walking with God also be deceived?

   The Christian not walking with God can also be deceived about what godly good is. He is deceived in thinking man seeks God, that there is some good in everyone, or that he has the ability on his own to affect non-Christians and bring about their salvation. Many do not know the degree to which they were once enslaved to sin and that even now Adam, or the old nature, is still in us and wants to stay in control.

5. Look at the list below that describes natural man. Select at least three words or phrases that best help you understand our spiritual condition before receiving Christ, and explain what they mean to you.

NATURAL MAN

- A sinner
- Condemned
- Devoid of the Spirit of God
- Slave to sin
- Has the nature of Satan
- Wants to do the desires of Satan
- Deaf to God
- Not of God
- Evil
- No resource (ability) to be godly

- No understanding of godly things
- Born in sin
- Cannot do spiritually good things
- Cannot please God
- Blind to God
- Has an evil heart
- Hostile, hater of God
- Unrighteous
- Does not seek God
- Spiritually dead

Personal answers.

6. a) Once God establishes us back into a relationship with Him, we are "in ___Christ___"; whereas before, we were "in _Adam_."

   b) The key difference between the two is this: When we were "in Adam," we were _slaves_ to sin. When we are "in Christ," we are set free from the _necessity_ to sin.

   c) Why do we still struggle with sin?

   We still have the "old Adam," or "old nature," or "flesh" in us. We may continue sinning rather than look to God to deliver us from our temptations and to change our hearts and minds, but it is because we choose not to live "in Christ."

7. a) What are four reasons why God wants us to know of our past depravity?

   The four reasons were:

   1) God wants us to know how horrible sin is so that we better understand the cost of what Jesus did for us on the cross. Understanding that Jesus "became sin" for us and died for our rebellion should help us see how valuable we are to God.

   2) Although beautiful and perfect, Adam and Eve were merely "creations" of God. When He redeemed us, God brought us into a position of "sons" or "children" of God—complete with all the inheritance that belongs to Jesus Christ. We are (in a way we really will not understand until we are with Him) becoming *one* with God. If we know how far away from Him we were, we can better understand the new position into which He placed us. We now are in God's eternal family. We are now joint-heirs with Christ, not just restored back to the high position of Adam and Eve before they rebelled.

   3) God wants us to know He is not mad at us and that He never punishes us. According to the dictionary, "punishment" means to inflict a penalty for an offense; it is to harm or hurt. Jesus Christ was punished for our sin. Although God may discipline us, He will never withhold His love. Discipline is to cause us to trust Him rather than our-

selves. He disciplines us to protect us—in the same way a loving parent disciplines a child so that she will learn to obey and not bring harm to herself.

4) The most important reason to know of our depravity is so we will have a healthy relationship with Him now. We must understand that we do not bring *any* godliness into our new relationship with Him. Spiritually, we come *totally bankrupt*. We are desperately dependent on God to share His goodness, His holiness, and His godliness with us. Our tendency is still to feel that we can bring some good to God—that we have the ability to do good things for Him and to help Him out. We often try to do things on our own or as a partner with God, and we fail. We need to know that *we have no adequacy in ourselves, but all our adequacy is from God* (2 Corinthians 3:5, PHILLIPS). *We need to know how desperately dependent* we must continue to be on Him for any godly or spiritual thing. *Apart from Him we can do nothing* (John 15:5)!

b) Which was the most significant to you and why?

Personal answers.

8. a) What two words best express how an understanding of the old nature still in us should affect how we live out our relationship with God (see page 82)?
   <u>Desperately</u> <u>dependent</u>

b) What words of Jesus reflect this principle (John 15:5)?

"Apart from Me you can do nothing."

9. In what areas do you find it hard to depend on God and why?

Personal answers.

10. If you were to share the information presented in this chapter with a friend, what main points would you communicate?

a) Humankind was created in the image of God (a reflection, not a duplicate) but with needs.

b) Because of Adam and Eve's rebellion, they died spiritually. They no longer had any personal relationship with God, and they lost His holiness and perfection.

c) Adam and Eve bore children, and all humankind since has been born in the image of Adam, which is completely without God's presence.

d) The non-Christian is totally blind and illogical about his spiritual deadness because sin has deceived him about his condition.

e) The non-Christian is a slave to sin, while the Christian is set free from the necessity to sin.

f) Four reasons God wants us to know our condition before becoming believers are:
- So that we will know how horrible sin is.
- Because of Christ's redemptive act for our sin, we are now in God's family—one with God—instead of being merely creations of God.
- God is not mad at us.
- Because "Adam" is still in us, and we must recognize our desperate dependency on God for anything spiritually good.

g) We must continually live in a relationship of desperate dependence on God to live a godly life.

11. From your journal page or highlighted text, what points—major or minor—were most significant to you and why?

Personal answers.

WHAT DOES IT MEAN TO ABIDE?

Primary Goal for Chapter 6

To be encouraged by the understanding that God has made a beautiful and amazing provision for us to live godly lives. In this chapter, we'll look at the means by which we are conformed to the image of Jesus Christ.

Overview

Abiding is submission to God with a willingness to trust Him with all the circumstances we face. In practice, it is being aware of God's presence, being available and obedient to Him, and trusting in His resources instead of our own. Although we still struggle with sin, God has made a provision for us to be free from the *control* it can still have over us. We will look at:

1. God's provision for relationship with us
2. How that changes us

1. What is the provision God has made for us, through His Son, for an intimate relationship?
   - Jesus came into the world to be the visible expression of the invisible God (Colossians 1:15). He provides us a "life line" with God the Father and a model of total dependence on the Father (John 5:30).
   - Before God redeemed us, we were spiritually dead, like a dead stick that takes a miracle to bring to life.
   - He grafts each of us in our deadness (sin nature) into Himself (the Vine). Now we (the branches) have new life—His life (His nature)—running through us, creating His fruit (fruit of the Spirit).

- An abiding relationship is one of dependency, not partnership. The fruit that we bear is evidence of His life in us.
- He is not merely "helping" us to be or do what He intends; He is producing the fruit (His own character traits) in us. His life replaces our deadness.

2. How does this provision for relationship change us?
   - As we abide in Christ we realize that, even as Christians, we do not have any human capacity to be godly on our own. We are freed from trying to change ourselves and produce the fruit of the Spirit on our own.
   - As we abide in Him, we begin to trust God and His resources for our lives.
   - As we abide in Him, we begin to recognize the body of Christ as our "family" with "one heart" (Ezekiel 11:19–20).
   - God has placed the Holy Spirit in our lives to guide and change us, and as we abide in Him we become more and more sensitive to His presence. He has given us a measure of free will, however, and we can choose to abide or not abide, to quench or not quench the Spirit. If we do quench the Spirit and stray away from the Lord, He may discipline us to bring us back to Himself.
   - As we abide in Christ, He shares His thoughts and feelings with us so we have "the mind of Christ" (Philippians 2:5).
   - As we abide in Christ, He purges the deadness of our sin nature and replaces it with His life and character (conforming us to the image of Jesus Christ, Romans 8:28–29). Many times this purging comes through very difficult struggles in which God can demonstrate Himself to us. Joseph is a biblical example of how God used what seemed to be unfair events for Joseph's good. We can see during his reign in Egypt how Joseph had taken on the "likeness of Christ" in the way he treated his brothers.

Points to Emphasize

Jesus has grafted us into Himself and sealed the union (Philippians 1:6). If we choose to abide, He will purge out our human deadness and replace it with His character or likeness—the fruit of the Spirit. We will be set free from the control of sin.

Possible Issues

Although some of the verses might bring up issues of election and free will, this probably will be the last chapter in which these topics come up. Please put these topics aside. You should not encounter many questions about the content of this chapter.

Discussion Questions and Possible Answers

The questions in this chapter are focused on abiding and the fruit of the Spirit. Because John 15:1–5 is so significant to this chapter, you might open your discussion time by having someone read those verses. Questions 1, 3, 5a, 5b, and 6 are "head knowledge"—facts that you will want your group to know and understand. The remaining questions are application.

As the facilitator, read the gray sidebar on page 96 called "Rooted in the Vine," and ask God to make it real to you. In any kind of discipleship relationship, it is very easy for the person leading to get sidetracked by a desire to feel significant, often without realizing it. As leaders, we have to abide and seek God to direct our own lives. And we must encourage the individuals in our group to abide and look to God, not to us.

1. a) What is the "fruit" (evidence that the Spirit lives within you) referred to in John 15?

    It is the fruit of the Spirit described in Galatians 5:22–23: *"The fruit of the Spirit is love, joy, peace, patience, kindness, goodness, faithfulness, gentleness, self-control."* This is the character and nature of God.

    b) Who produces it?

    The Vine—Jesus Christ—produces the fruit as we abide. Many people think *they* are responsible for producing the fruit in their lives, as opposed to abiding in Christ and *letting Him produce the fruit.* As the members of your group understand the life of Christ in them, hopefully they will experience freedom from guilt about performance and failure and experience a hunger to pursue an abiding relationship with the Lord. Growth is an ongoing process.

2. Following are some opposites of the fruit of the Spirit (listed in Galatians 5:22–23). You may think of others to add. a) Circle the ones that you struggle with, and b) write down specific circumstances that illicit these responses.

    Love: anger, hate, sarcasm, ridicule, disdain, avoidance, indifference, bitterness, self-centeredness, resentment, jealousy, lust, judgmental attitude, manipulation

    Joy: fear, sadness, depression, self-pity, sorrow, dejection, loneliness, doubt, discontentment, apathy

    Peace: anxiety, worry, nervousness, fear, conflict, hostility, drivenness, turmoil, guilt, discontentment, frustration, envy, insecurity, disillusionment, people-pleasing

    Patience: irritation, frustration, restlessness, complaining, agitation, whining, short-temperedness

    Kindness: rudeness, superior attitude, harshness, ignoring other people, sarcasm, cutting remarks, selfishness, meanness, unforgiveness, hurtful, condescending, inconsiderate, false-flattery

    Goodness: ego, pride, selfishness, being hurtful or abusive, corrupt, jealous, rebellious, evil, deceitful, envious, unmerciful, idolatrous, disrespectful, lying, stealing, crude language

    Faithfulness: not keeping your word or commitments, untrustworthy, compromising, infidelity, gossiping, disloyal, backstabbing, betrayal, fickleness, deceitful, adultery

    Gentleness: insensitive, cutting, brutally frank, physically or verbally abusive, severe, harsh, domineering, callous, rude, sarcastic, vengeful, aggressive, no compassion, tactless

Self-control: undisciplined, little willpower or restraint, indulgent, disobedient, impulsive, disrespectful, obsessive, addictions, lust, unfocused, procrastination, immorality, drunkenness, losing your temper

a) Personal answers.

This question helps identify what is *not* the fruit of the Spirit in our lives and points out areas in which we need Christ to change us. It is very important for each member of your group to share from some or all of the list. Sharing our weaknesses bonds us together and allows us to pray for one another. This exercise can be discouraging, but remind your group that all of us struggle with our old nature and that we are all in the *process* of being conformed to Christ.

b) Personal answers.

Hopefully by now your group members will feel comfortable with each other and be willing to share their answers. We all have things from this list that we struggle with, and they often occur under certain circumstances. If your group is reticent, consider sharing some of your own list first.

c) In what areas do you see God changing you so that you more often display His character?

Personal answers.

This question should be an encouragement. Have your group look for areas in which there has been growth in their lives. If they don't see change and you do, be sure to point it out. Our changed lives are one of the greatest proofs to us of the existence of God.

3. a) What does "Apart from Me you can do nothing" mean?

In our humanness we can do nothing godly, spiritual, or of eternal significance.

b) Give some examples.

Questions 3a and 3b remind us that, although we can do good in this world—things that pertain to time and space—we can do nothing of spiritual significance. Apart from Him, we cannot do godly things or become like Christ. Be sure to have your group give some concrete examples, such as producing godly character (the fruit of the Spirit), ministry, having God's mind on decisions, selfless giving, and loving. We cannot produce peace, patience, or joy on our own. God has to do it for us. In ministry, we can only point people to the Lord, what He has done, and what He is doing. *He* has to work in the hearts of others to make this truth real to them. We can make decisions on our own, but unless they are prompted by God, they will not have any bearing on a deepening relationship with the Lord.

4. a) Define "abiding."

   Abiding is our decision and our desire to depend on God, trusting Him with the circumstances we face and being available to Him for prompting, transforming, and leading. This question is important for your group to grapple with.

   b) How do you personally know when you are abiding and when you are not?

   Personal answers.

   We are abiding when our heart's desire is to be in a trusting relationship with God and to let Him change us. Although we will not be without sin, we will recognize our dependency on Him to handle temptation, and we will accept His mercy and grace when we do sin. We will be in communication with Him: thanking Him, asking for His mind and attitudes on things, seeking His direction, and spending time in His Word. We can be more obedient to His commands, and we will begin to see the fruit of the Spirit in our lives. We will recognize that He is changing us.

   The question of whether we can sin while abiding may come up. We are imperfect people, in the *process* of being conformed to the image of Christ. The instinctive sinful thought or response can happen when we are abiding, and we can struggle with following the Lord. But when God reminds us of our sin and we hear His voice, it is great evidence that we *are* abiding.

   When we are actively rebellious to Scripture and God's prompting, when we trust ourselves and leave Him out of our lives, or when we have no desire to spend time with Him, we are not abiding. We will see the opposites of the fruit of the Spirit in our lives, and we may experience discipline from God.

   c) Where are you right now?

   Personal answers.

5. a) What does "purge" mean?

   Purge means to clean out something, usually bad, and replace it with something new.

   b) If you are abiding, God is in the process of purging the ___deadness___ from your life.

   c) List the things that most need purging from your life. (Consider your answers to Question 2 as well as other attitudes or lifestyle choices.)

   Personal answers.

   In addition to the opposites in Question 2, God may purge a "do-it-yourself" attitude (lack of trust), filthy thoughts and language, sexual promiscuity, unhealthy habits, lying, rebellion toward authority, and other sin.

6. a) What is God's purpose for our lives—the "good" described in Romans 8:28–29?

God's purpose is to conform us to the image of Jesus Christ, to give Himself (His character) to us, producing the fruit of the Spirit, or His likeness, in our lives. Keep reminding your group of this.

b) Why does God often use difficult circumstances to produce this good?

We know that the producing of God's "good" in our lives is not always pleasant or comfortable. Circumstances that are not good from our point of view may be part of God's "conforming" purposes in our lives. The difficult situations may force us to trust God, to recognize that He is in control of all things—even things that we do not understand and that do not seem good to us. We often need tough and difficult circumstances to realize how desperately we need God and to deal with our pride. In easy circumstances, our tendency is to try to handle things ourselves.

You may want to refer your group to the top of page 102 about circumstances that can just as easily produce the opposite of the fruit of the Spirit.

7. List specific ways in which you are living (or have lived) as though you were in a "partnership" or "independent-contractor" relationship with God.

You may have to explain that an independent contractor makes all his own decisions and relies on his own resources. This do-it-yourself, make-your-own-decisions attitude is very prevalent in our culture and has crept into the Christian way of thinking. It is important to constantly evaluate if we are *following* the Lord's direction and *depending* on Him in the same way Jesus modeled His submissiveness to the Father.

Ask for specific examples. Christians often decide on their own what ministry or activity they will do for God, then ask Him to "bless" it. They decide whom they will witness to and what they should say. They will try to act out the fruit of the Spirit on their own and try to obey the commands of Scripture in their own strength.

8. If you were to share the information presented in this chapter with a friend, what main points would you communicate?

a) Apart from the Vine (Jesus Christ) we can, in our humanness, do nothing spiritual, godly, or eternally significant.

b) God is committed (Philippians 1:6) to conform us to His image (Romans 8:29)—to produce the fruit of the Spirit (His character or nature) in us. Only God can accomplish this.

c) Abiding is the desire to depend on God and to be available to His prompting, transforming, and leading.

d) God has given us "one" heart—His heart.

e) We can, with our new measure of free will, quench the Spirit and not abide.

f) God must "purge" our deadness to produce in us the fruit of the Spirit and conform us to His image. This may sometimes involve difficult circumstances that force us to trust Him.

9. From your journal page or highlighted text, what points—major or minor—were most significant to you and why?

Personal answers.

Please Note: Before you end this meeting, you may want to have your group turn to Question 7 in the next chapter. People sometimes have a hard time understanding what to do with this question. If you have time, ask your group to turn to this question and explain it, possibly by reading the example in this Leader's Guide (see pages 49 and 50).

WHAT IS MY PART AND WHAT IS GOD'S PART?

Primary Goal of Chapter 7

To understand our responsibility and God's provision in our relationship with Him.

Overview

This chapter deals in depth with Romans 12:1–2, which urges us to present ourselves to God as a living and holy sacrifice, acceptable to Him (through Christ), as an act of worship, then explains what God has to do for us. We cannot understand why presenting ourselves to God is necessary for a biblical relationship with the Lord unless we have a true understanding of the nature of God and ourselves, as outlined in the previous six chapters of the study.

In this chapter we will look at:
1. What is our responsibility in our relationship with God?
2. What is God's commitment to us to help us live in relationship with Him?
3. What does it mean to present ourselves, and what problems do we run into when we present?

1. What is our responsibility in our relationship with God?
   - This passage's two active verbs are "present" and "prove," meaning we have to do them.

- Because we understand who God is and what He has done for us (His mercy), we are to present ourselves to Him. This means we merely have to "step forward" and offer ourselves to God. This requires an understanding of how desperately dependent we are on Him to conform us to His likeness.
- By knowing that we are already "holy and acceptable" to God because of Christ's substitutionary death for us, we can freely present all the ugliness in our lives to Him.
- Presenting is not dependent on our emotions but on our knowledge of who God is and what He has done for us. He is more interested in *us* than the *circumstances* that we are often engrossed with. In faith we focus not on the *circumstances,* but on the *Master of all circumstances.* We can ask God to make understanding real in our hearts, not just in our heads.
- Presenting is an act of trust because we recognize that God is in control and loves us. It is, therefore, our highest form of worship ("spiritual service of worship," Romans 12:1).
- Presenting is the only way to prove or discover the will of God for our lives.

2. What is God's commitment to us?
   - "Be (not) conformed" and "be transformed" are passive verbs, meaning God has to do these for us.
   - He is in the process of "unconforming" us from the world (and the spiritual deadness we brought into our relationship with Him).
   - He transforms us into the likeness of Christ. He renews our minds, changing our thoughts, attitudes, and emotions, which affects the way we act. This metamorphosis is a process. *He alone can change us.* He wants to give us His nature, but we have to give up our control to gain His control.
   - When we present, He acts in and for us so we *know* we are in His will.

3. What does it mean to present ourselves, and what kinds of problems do we run into when we present?
   - God wants us to present everything—specifically areas in which the world has a hold on us and in which we need Him to transform us into His likeness. He wants us on the altar so He can transform our very nature.
   - In the process of presenting, we struggle in the following ways:
     - One foot on, one foot off the altar—presenting things to the Lord with conditions.
     - Falling off the altar—presenting things to the Lord, then going back to our old habits and trying to take care of things ourselves.
     - Jumping off the altar—presenting things to the Lord, but not trusting His timing and taking back control.

Points to Emphasize

Our part in an intimate relationship with the Lord is to present every aspect of our lives to Him. If we present ourselves, God's promise is to "unconform" us from the world system and transform us into the likeness of Christ by giving us His mind. Only God can do this, and this should be great, freeing news. Make sure your group thoroughly understands Romans 12:1–2, two verses crucial to understanding how our relationship with God is meant to be lived.

Possible Issues

Although the discussion of the grammar in Romans 12:1–2 may be new to many, there should not be any major problems or issues in this chapter.

Discussion Questions and Possible Answers

The questions in this chapter deal with both "head knowledge" and "heart knowledge." Questions 1 and 3 are designed to make sure that everyone in the group accurately understands Romans 12:1–2.

Question 2 helps us see how we are already conformed to the world, and it encourages us to pinpoint areas of our life that we need to present to the Lord. Some people think they have to clean themselves up before they can have a "good" relationship with God. Emphasize to your group that we are all in process throughout our entire life and the Lord desires to have a growing relationship with us during this process.

Most people will say that they struggle at different times with all of the problems listed in Question 4. Questions 5 and 6 are extensions of this discussion. Encourage your group members to share something personal they are presenting to the Lord right now and to describe how they struggle with presenting.

Question 7 is an exercise to help each individual make the truth of God's Word real in his or her heart. Some people will not understand what is asked for in this question or may think they have to give a "right" answer. Encourage them to let God speak to their hearts through these verses. If someone in your group did not understand this question, encourage them to work on it later on their own. The personalizing of these two verses has been extremely meaningful to many people.

1. The four verbs in Romans 12:1–2 that pertain to us are: present, be (not) conformed, be transformed, and prove.

   a) Which are active (the subject does the action) and which are passive (the subject receives the action)? In other words, what can we do, and what do we have to have done for us?

      Present and *prove* are active. *Be not conformed* and *be transformed* are passive.

   b) From what we learned about the spiritual condition of natural man, why do the two passive verbs (be not conformed and be transformed) have to be passive?

      Natural man is spiritually blind, spiritually deaf, and spiritually dead. Romans 3:11 also says that *no one* has ever sought a relationship with God. On our own, we do not have the ability or desire to become godly. Jesus said that apart from Him we can do *nothing,* and we are desperately dependent on Him for anything spiritual in our lives. We cannot "unconform" ourselves from the world and the deadness that held us, and we cannot transform ourselves or have God's mind on our own. He must do this for us. We must present ourselves so that God can act on our behalf. Presenting is our responsibility and our opportunity.

   c) How does understanding these verbs change the way you understood Romans 12:1–2 in the past?

Personal answers.

Without understanding these verbs, many people thought they commanded us to disengage ourselves from the world and transform our minds on our own. They thought we had to change ourselves by modeling our actions after Jesus.

2. We are already conformed to a worldly perspective in many areas.

a) Whether a person has many possessions or few, what attitudes about material things are wrong?

Material things are not, in themselves, bad. When they become our primary focus, when they are the source of our significance (pride) or our security, or when accumulating wealth or the fear of losing it controls us, then our *attitude* about material things is wrong. These attitudes replace our honor of, thankfulness to, and dependence on God as our continual provider.

b) What worldly possessions and desires are important to you?

Personal answers.

In our materialistic world, many people believe their significance and security lie in having things: houses, clothes, cars, good jobs, education, status, power, respect. Some important desires people may have are marriage, children, careers, beauty/fitness, good health.

c) In what specific ways have you been influenced by the values portrayed in movies, TV, music, advertising, and other media?

Personal answers.

A lot of the media portray ungodly attitudes about sexual activity, profanity and vulgarity, honesty, faithfulness to marriage or other relationships. Ask your group members if they have become desensitized to ungodly language and values.
   We have been conditioned to view our importance and our value by how attractive we are, how intelligent or talented we are, how successful we are, how much money we have, or how much power we have. These worldly values and goals are promoted by various forms of media and can promote serious problems such as poor body image and eating disorders.

d) In what way, if any, do you think the world's perspective has influenced churches and other Christian ministries? If you are involved in some form of ministry, how have your ministry methods and attitudes been influenced by the world?

Churches and Christian organizations often operate just like businesses, using the world's system of gaining support, setting goals, and advertising. They often approach growth from the world's perspective of how to attract people. We frequently think that if we are more professional or more sophisticated in our approach, more people will come to God. We falsely believe that God needs us and our strategies. (How many marketing executives would have had God come to earth as a baby rather than as an attractive man of talent and authority? What methods might we use today?)

The second part of the question will be personal answers. Some in your group may not have been involved in any kind of ministry. Make sure they don't feel uncomfortable.

e) Look at your answers to the four parts of this question. List the areas in which you need the Lord to "unconform" you from the world's perspective and give you His perspective.

Personal answers.

3. Why is presenting ourselves an act of worship?

When we present something to God, we trust Him and recognize who He is. When we present, we trust that God cares about our needs, that He has the wisdom to know what is best, and that He has the ability to do something about it. It is an act of worship to acknowledge these things about God by actively presenting our concerns to Him. This is called lordship.

4. We looked at three difficulties with being a living sacrifice. Are you now experiencing, or have you ever experienced, any of the problems listed below? Be specific and include reasons you do (or did) this.

a) One foot on the altar, one on the ground (presenting with conditions attached)

Personal answers.

This is when we partially give something to God but want to retain some control. It is deciding on our own initiative what we will do or what we want to do, then asking God to bless us and give us the power or ability to do it. For example, we might give something to God, but we also tell Him how we want Him to answer or how soon we want Him to answer. Bargaining with God—telling Him we will do something if He will do something in return—would also fall into this category.

b) Climbing on the altar, and then falling off (presenting a problem, then later finding yourself worrying about it)

Personal answers.

We seriously want to trust the Lord with something but later find that, although not necessarily intentionally, we have taken it back. It will often be in areas in which we are anxious or worried about something. We present our problem to the Lord and trust Him with it, but later we start to worry again. Or perhaps we want to be completely dependent on Him but later find ourselves taking the initiative ourselves.

If we soon realize that we're trying to take back control and we present it again to the Lord, it is a good sign that we are abiding. God prompted us to give it back to Him and trust Him with it. If we continue trying to handle it on our own anyway, we move away from an abiding posture.

   c) Getting on the altar, then jumping off (giving something to God, then consciously taking back control)

   Personal answers.

   We see this most often in major areas in which we feel insecure and fearful: in dating or marriage relationships, job or career opportunities, or finances. One reason we jump back off the altar is *God's timing*. If He doesn't act immediately, it is hard to trust Him any longer. Sometimes we fear that He will not, or cannot, act for us. (Refer to Jesus' trusting the Father with His temptation in the wilderness.)

5. Make a list of things you need to present right now.

   Personal answers.

6. Are there things you are not willing to present? Why?

   Personal answers. Do not put anyone on the spot.

   If there are things that your group members are not willing to present, try to help them understand why. Perhaps they do not fully understand what God's good for us is, or they still think they are responsible for producing fruit in their life. Typically we are unwilling to present something to God because we think the process will be too difficult, not realizing that as we depend on Him we take on His nature and ability to change. Chapter 8 discusses further what God intends in this metamorphosis of our nature.

7. Using your own words, rewrite Romans 12:1–2 as if it were a letter from God to you. Try to include key concepts and words.

   I urge you therefore, brethren, by the mercies of God, to present your bodies a living and holy sacrifice, acceptable to God, which is your spiritual service of worship. And do not be conformed to this world, but be transformed by the renewing of your mind, that you may prove what the will of God is, that which is good and acceptable and perfect.

   Following is an explanation of each phrase. Your group's answers will be more personalized and will not include all of this. See the example of a personalized paraphrase on the following page. If some in your group misunderstand this question and simply define each phrase, ask them to rewrite the two verses later as a letter to them from God. This can be a meaningful exercise.

   I urge you—God does not force us to present ourselves; rather, He urges or begs us because He has re-established a love relationship that involves choice. He knows it is for our good, and it is absolutely necessary for a growing relationship with Him.

therefore—Refers to what has been said up until this verse. Before he asks us to *do* anything, Paul uses 11 chapters to cover the major themes: our significance to God, who God is, what sin has done to us and the condition of natural man, God's purpose for believers, and our inheritance (His provision for leading a godly life).

brethren—This instruction is only to believers. Your group should insert their own name.

by the mercies of God—God paid for our sin by the death of Jesus Christ through which He brought us into a relationship with Him. It was mercy because He was under no obligation to do it. He chose to do it because of His love. *Nothing* can keep us from His love.

to present your bodies—We are to present to God the total essence of who we are—everything about us, whether good or bad. It is our minds, our emotions or feelings, our attitudes, and our circumstances.

a living—We are a living sacrifice because we can be in a continual, ongoing relationship with God. We have the ability to abide or not abide, to trust Him or to do things on our own initiative.

and holy sacrifice, acceptable to God—We do not have to *become* "holy"—to clean up our lives—before we can present something to God or before we are acceptable to Him. Positionally we are already holy and acceptable to God—just the way we are—because Jesus Christ paid for our sins. Jesus said in John 15:3 that we are clean already.

which is your spiritual service of worship—Presenting ourselves is our act of worship because we honor God by acknowledging our dependence on Him for all change and spiritual good.

And do not be conformed to this world—Do not let the world *continue* to hold us captive to its attitudes. Conformed is a passive verb. God must do it for us. We were already conformed to the world when we came into our relationship with God. He wants to move us out of this slavery and purge our deadness.

but be transformed by the renewing of your mind—Be transformed is also passive. God is the one who must transform us or conform us to the image of Jesus Christ. He renews our mind by giving us His thoughts and attitudes.

that you may prove what the will of God is, that which is good and acceptable and perfect—When we present ourselves to God to transform us, everything we do *will* be God's will for us. As we abide and present, God directs us and we live out His will. God's will is always for our good, the good of conforming us to the image of Jesus Christ. As He transforms us, we will have His mind and, therefore, will think and act in the way He wants us to.

Example of a personal paraphrase:

"Because I love you, I plead with you, Whitney, as my dear child, by the overflowing grace I am filled with, to climb on my lap and surrender your essence and soul—a live testimony and a witness of my power—a surrendering of all that you are, which is how you show your love, trust, and obedience to Me alone. And do not allow the flesh of the world to bind you, but allow Me to change you and give you My mind. This is the only way to truly know what I want for your life, Whitney, and to understand what is good in My sight, what I want to bless you with, and what is the perfect way for Me to complete you and finish the work I have started. I love you."

(Romans 12:1–2 paraphrase by Whitney Schnacke Mounts)

8. If you were to share the information presented in this chapter with a friend, what main points would you communicate?

   a) We have one primary responsibility in our new relationship with God—to present everything about ourselves to Him.

   b) If we present ourselves to God, He promises to "unconform" us from the world system and transform us into the likeness of Christ. We cannot do this ourselves; He has to do it for us.

   c) It is an act of worship to present things to God because it shows our trust in Him.

   d) When we present, we are automatically in God's will because He is transforming us and giving us His mind.

   e) Transformation is a lifelong process.

9. From your journal page or highlighted text, what points—major or minor—were most significant to you and why?

   Personal answers.

   Many people have felt they had to clean up their lives to be acceptable to God. Some have misunderstood these verses and thought they commanded them to—on their own—disentangle themselves from the world system and transform themselves into Christ's likeness. They believed *they* were responsible for modifying their behavior (perhaps with God's help), rather than letting *God* transform them.

   I hope this is an extremely freeing chapter and that it clarifies what we need to do in our relationship with God and what He has promised to do in us and for us.

HOW SHOULD I RESPOND TO DIFFICULT CIRCUMSTANCES?

Primary Goal of Chapter 8

To realize that God wants to penetrate and transform the core of who we are. He wants us to present *everything* about ourselves: our circumstances, our emotions, and most important, our attitudes.

Overview

This chapter continues to help us understand God's purpose for us—*to become like Christ*—and what that looks like in our lives. Our responsibility is to be in a daily abiding relationship with God through the Vine (Jesus Christ), recognizing that He is our source of life. Chapter 8 helps us understand that: 1) God is transforming our hearts, and 2) He does this over time.

1. How is God transforming our hearts?
   - He is more interested in our heart attitudes than our circumstances. He cares about the daily circumstances we encounter, but His purpose is greater than protecting us from all difficult experiences. He uses everything that happens to us to bring us into an abiding

and dependent relationship with Him.

- He wants us to present more than our circumstances to Him. He also wants us to present more than our emotions, which are a response to our circumstances. God wants us to present our underlying *attitudes*. It is not always easy for us to recognize our attitudes, but if we ask Him, God wants to help us identify the self-centeredness that causes us to react in the ways we do.
- The account of Paul and Silas in the Philippian jail is a good illustration of how God's transformation of our attitudes can affect the way we respond to situations.
- Philippians 4:6–7 tells us to present our anxious circumstances and emotions to the Lord with an *attitude* of submission to what He knows is best (supplication). We should thank Him that He is good, that He loves us, that He is in control. Then He will give us His mind and attitudes—a peace even if we have no understanding.

2. The transformation of our hearts will happen over time.
- We are "positionally" perfect because of Christ's death for us, but the transformation of our attitudes and character is a process.
- Even when our desire is to abide, we can still act or think imperfectly. If we are aware of this sin, it is evidence that we *are* abiding because we have felt the conviction of the Holy Spirit.
- God has to continually give us wisdom, direction, love, peace, and everything else we need. There is no other source.
- The process of transformation is a necessary blessing that keeps us in a dependent relationship with the Lord. He wants a growing relationship with us.
- Once we present our desire to abide, God plays a major role in helping us continue to abide (Philippians 1:6).

Points to Emphasize

We are now looking at practical areas in our lives that we should present—especially the underlying attitudes that make us respond the way we do. Remind your group to ask the Lord to reveal these things. Make sure your group really understands Philippians 4:6–7, especially the meaning of supplication: an attitude of complete submission to whatever God knows is best.

Possible Issues

There should not be any major issues raised.

Discussion Questions and Possible Answers

Please Note: Because these questions involve a great deal of personal application, you may need more than one session to adequately cover them.

The questions in this chapter focus on our continued understanding of our responsibility in our relationship with God: *We present. He transforms.*

Question 1 helps us understand the difference between our circumstances, emotions, and attitudes, while Questions 2 and 3 help us identify the ways we tend to focus on circumstances instead of attitudes.

Supplication, addressed in Question 4, is important to understand so that we know what our attitude should be when we pray. Question 5 is another opportunity to hear from God individually as we personalize His Word—Philippians 4:6–7—to us. (This is the same exercise as Question 7 in the previous chapter.) This is very helpful to internalize Scripture and allow God to make His Word real in our hearts. Encourage each member of your group to do this exercise.

For those in your group who have experienced the peace described in Question 6, it should be an encouragement that God is very much present in their lives.

Encourage your group members that recognizing attitudes is half the battle, but the process of presenting these attitudes to Christ to change usually does not happen overnight. They should not be discouraged if they have to present over and over. Ungodly attitudes may be deeply ingrained, and we battle constantly with our old nature. God wants us to be constantly dependent on Him, and He reveals His grace and mercy throughout the process of conforming us to His image.

1. a) Using the headings on the next page, list specific circumstances that provoke negative emotions or responses in you. (To refresh your memory, review your answers to Question 2 in Chapter 6.)

   b) Now list the attitudes that might be the cause of each response you listed. (We don't always know our underlying attitudes. Below are some attitudes that may help you answer.)

I want to be in control of (all situations) (people around me).
I want my own way.
People should (think like I do) (act like I do) (believe what I do).
No one has the right to tell me what to do.
I am (better than) (smarter than) (more educated than) (more organized than) others.
This is the way I am . . . just deal with it!
I don't want to be around people who are different from me.
I need (friends) (a boyfriend/girlfriend) (a spouse) (children) (money) (sex) (a house) (a car) (nice clothes) to be happy.
I have a right to be (happy) (comfortable) (pain free).
It is my right to correct or change other people because I know what is best.
I am owed something because (I've done so much) (I've had it so bad) (others have more than I do).
I must do whatever it takes to get what I want.
My value is in (what I own) (my looks) (my intelligence) (who I know) (what I can do for others).
Compared to others, (I don't know as much) (I'm not as talented) (I don't have as much).
I need the approval of other people.
If anything bad is going to happen, it will happen to me.
I'm afraid to be my real self.
I have to do everything perfectly.
I'm responsible for other people's problems.
Commitments are unimportant to me if something better comes along.

CIRCUMSTANCES	EMOTIONS/ RESPONSES	ATTITUDES
Disagreement with coworker	Anger	People should think like I do.

Personal answers. This is a difficult question to answer. Here are some more examples that may help people understand:

The boss criticized my work.	Defensiveness Depression, self-pity	• I'm smarter than he is. • I have to do everything perfectly. • I need the approval of others.
A woman at the party had a beautiful outfit.	Envy	I have to have nice clothes to be happy.
A person with a handicap came to our meeting.	Avoided and ignored the person	I don't want to be around people who are different from me.

Pray that this will be a good time of self-examination of attitudes that need God's transforming work and that the group will share and discuss freely.

We have to understand the difference between our circumstances, emotions, and attitudes. *God is intent on changing us on the inside and giving us His attitudes.* We may be only asking Him to change our circumstances. It is often difficult to identify the attitudes behind an emotion or circumstance. Help your group talk through personal examples together using the guidelines in Question 1. The attitudes listed in this question are negative to make us aware of the attitudes we should present to God to change. We can, however, have positive attitudes (the attitudes of Christ) as God changes our nature. For instance, an attitude that we hope to take from this study is that God is using all things to conform us to the likeness of Christ (Romans 8:28–29). This attitude allows us to praise Him in the midst of all situations, as was reflected in the story of Paul and Silas in prison (Acts 16:22–30).

2. What kind of new circumstances do you tend to create to override bad circumstances?

Personal answers.

People may run to sympathetic friends or use the diversions of eating, music, TV/videos, novels, movies, exercise, drugs, alcohol, or sleep.

3. a) Are there circumstances, habits, or emotions in your life that are so strong or overwhelming that they hold you captive? What are they?

Personal answers.

It could be things like pride, anger, lust, insecurities, depression, self-esteem, coveting—anything that is opposite of the fruit of the Spirit. Any situation that consumes a great deal of our thoughts is holding us captive.

b) Were there things in the past that held you captive but no longer do? If so, what?

Personal answers.

This is one of the greatest evidences of the reality and existence of God and His love for us. When we see godly changes in our lives and attitudes, we should give thanks and rejoice that He gives His character to us.

c) What are you anxious about right now? In what ways do you deal with your anxiousness?

Personal answers.

At this point in the study, your group members should seriously evaluate whether they are presenting anxious situations to the Lord and receiving His peace, or if they continue to worry and focus on their circumstances.

4. What does "supplication" mean? Give an example of how you could pray with supplication.

Supplication is an attitude of total surrender to whatever God knows is best for conforming us to His image. It is trust—a "whatever, Lord" response, with no conditions attached. An example of praying with supplication would be: "Lord, my desire in this situation is that You would [fill in the blank]. But I am confident that You know what is best, and I will trust You no matter how You choose to answer."

5. Using your own words, rewrite Philippians 4:6–7 as a letter from God to you. Try to include key concepts and words.

Be anxious for nothing, but in everything by prayer and supplication with thanksgiving let your requests be made known to God. And the peace of God, which surpasses all comprehension, shall guard your hearts and your minds in Christ Jesus.

Your group should come up with a *personal* version of these two verses, similar to what they did with Romans 12:1–2 in the previous chapter. Make sure they include and understand supplication.

6. Have you ever experienced peace without understanding? Give specifics.

Personal answers.

God does not promise that our circumstances will always be pleasant and peaceful, but He can give peace that is unnatural during difficult circumstances. God's peace is a calmness of thought, attitude, and emotion—often in the midst of very trying circumstances. The stress that affects our whole bodies will be absent. God's peace gives us the ability to accept things without second-guessing Him, the confidence that He is in control of the circumstance and that He loves us. Peace is often irrational, from a human standpoint, in the face of negative circumstances. We may still experience the emotions of sadness and loss about distressing and painful things. But the underlying sense that God loves us, knows what is best, is in control, and is conforming us to His image gives us an assurance that what is happening will be for our eternal good.

It's easier to have peace when we know the reason for hard circumstances. God promises to give us peace even when we have no understanding of the reason for the situation.

Peace is not like a drink of cool water that we enjoy while it lasts and then ask God for more when it runs out. Peace is a *person. Jesus Christ is peace.* He lives within us and shares His own character, nature, and confidence with us. He will actually share His mind, or attitude of peacefulness, with us.

7. If you were to share the information presented in this chapter with a friend, what main points would you communicate?

a) "Presenting" means to turn over to God the control of our circumstances, emotions, and attitudes. Attitudes are the most important. This is the primary area of our lives that God conforms to His image by producing in us the fruit of the Spirit.

b) When we are in tense situations, we are to pray or present our situation and emotions to God with thanksgiving and supplication. Supplication is to pray in total trust and surrender to what God knows is best in the situation.

c) If we present our anxious situation to God with supplication, He promises to give us peace, even if we do not understand why the circumstances are happening.

8. From your journal page or highlighted text, what points—major or minor—were most significant to you and why?

Personal answers.

HOW CAN I KNOW GOD'S WILL FOR MY LIFE?

Primary Goal of Chapter 9

To give people confidence that if they are abiding, presenting, and truly desiring God's will, they can trust Him to give direction.

Overview

This chapter addresses knowing and walking with God as Jesus instructed in John 15:7:

"If you abide in Me, and My words abide in you, ask whatever you wish, and it shall be done for you."

The major topics in this chapter are:
1. God has a *general will* for all believers.
2. He also has a *specific will* for each of us.
3. What is *our responsibility* in knowing and walking in God's will?

1. God's general will for all Christians is to know Him through His Word, as instructed in "and My words abide in you."
   - We seek to know God and ourselves through His written Word. The truest thing about

God is what He says about Himself, and the truest thing about us is what He says about us.
- Along with other instruction in Scripture, God puts great emphasis on abiding and presenting.
- The commands and principles in Scripture are for all believers, but they are only *one part* of God's will.

2. God has a specific will for each of us, a unique path on which He guides us in individual ways to conform us to the likeness of Christ, as instructed in "If you abide in Me."
   - In addition to knowing and following Scripture, Jesus says to "Come follow Me"—to submit to God's leading and provision for our needs. As illustrated in the account of the rich young ruler, there is no "Plan B."
   - We see the submission of Jesus, Paul, and others to God's personal will.
   - When we abide, God promises to direct our steps in ways that are good for us and to use this journey to conform us to the image of Christ.
   - God has a specific will for us in regard to where we go or what we do if it affects our growing relationship with Him and with others.
   - When we abide and present, God reveals His personal will to us through a) *circumstances,* b) giving us His *mind and desires,* and 3) *peace.*
   - When we abide and present, we will automatically be in God's will. We cannot make a wrong turn because He will direct or redirect us.
   - One of the greatest ways we can worship God is to step out in faith, believing that He will lead us where He wants us to go and in what He wants us to do. But we often see His leading only in hindsight.

3. What is our responsibility in knowing God's will?
   - We must have an attitude of trust and submission to a loving and sovereign God who knows what is best for us.
   - We often ask: "What does God want me to do?" or "Where does God want me to go?" Instead, we should first ask, "Do I really trust God and want His will, whatever it may be?" His leading involves more than our actions. It is for the greater purpose of transforming us.
   - The question is not so much, "How do I know God's will?" but rather, "Am I abiding and presenting, and do I trust God with my future?"

Points to Emphasize

God has a general will that applies to all of us, but He also has a specific, unique personal will for each individual. God's will involves what we do and where we go, but more important is who we are becoming and how it affects our growing relationship with Him and others. Three primary ways God leads us are through 1) circumstances, 2) giving us His thoughts and desires, and 3) peace. The important questions for us to ask ourselves are: "Am I abiding and presenting?" and "Do I truly want and trust God's leading for my future?"

Possible Issues

This chapter should not bring up many problems. Instead, I pray it will take away the uncertainty and anxiety many Christians have about how to know and walk in God's will.

Discussion Questions and Possible Answers

The questions in this chapter are meant to help people make application. We often look to people, organizations, or other things to meet our needs. Question 1 encourages us to identify what or whom we trust to meet our needs.

Questions 2 and 3 are designed to help the members of your group understand the difference between God's general will and His personal will in their lives. Help them see that *both* are necessary to know God's leading. Questions 4, 5, and 6 help us realize God's faithfulness to us.

Question 7a encourages us to discern how God guides us in a personal way, 7b looks at these methods in past circumstances, and 8 looks at present decisions.

Be sure to cover Question 9. The ability to trust our thoughts and heart desires because we are abiding is very freeing for people wanting to live in God's will.

1. a) Which people or what things have you looked to as the source, rather than the instrument, of meeting your needs?

   Personal answers.

   Younger people may look to parents, grandparents, jobs, or school loans. Later, many people look to their spouse, employers/companies, education, inheritance, or investment portfolios. People in ministry may look to the church or to donors for their support.

   b) Has this chapter changed your perspective? If so, how?

   Personal answers.

   Hopefully by this point in the study, people realize that God, because He is in control of all things, is the source of meeting our needs, even if He sometimes uses other people or other vehicles as the instrument.

2. a) What is the general will of God?

   The general will of God—which is the same for every Christian—is our knowledge of what God says to us in Scripture and our application of that to our lives. God commands us to study His Word and "hide it in our hearts" (know the content), so we need to be obedient in this area. The Bible contains many commands and instructions about what God wants us to do and not do. These are for all believers. He knows these areas of conduct are not only good, but they are a protection for us. If we do not know His instructions, we might think He wants us to do something that is totally against what He tells us in the Bible.

   b) What specifically are you doing to know God's general will?

   Personal answers.

   We all need to make every effort to spend time in the Word and be familiar with what it says. Group members should give specifics about how they are doing this—through personal study and quiet times, church attendance, group Bible studies, and other activities.

3. a) List current areas of your life in which you believe God has a specific will for you.

Personal answers.

God wants to direct us in events that involve our ongoing personal relationship with Him, as well as those that affect our relationships with other people. These events and relationships will involve and impact our own attitudes, and they are opportunities for Him to conform us.

b) Would God have an interest in what you wear or where you go today? If so, why?

Usually what clothes we wear, as long as they don't go against scriptural principles, would have no significance. It would only be important if, as mentioned in the illustration, what we wear is a result of an attitude we have.

It probably does not make any difference whether we go to the grocery store, or any other place, today or tomorrow. It would only matter if God wants us to be involved with a certain person while at the store or if He wants us to go at a certain time to encounter circumstances He will use in our lives.

God has a specific will in important choices about school, careers, the way we spend money, and so on. Even more important, He has a will in the area of our relationships: with friends, boyfriends/girlfriends, marriage partners, children, and parents. God most likely has a will in where we fellowship with other believers. And above all, He has a will regarding our nature—that we be conformed to the image of Jesus Christ. He has a will in how we treat others, what attitudes we have, how we speak, and how we think. God wants to change us to be like Him.

4. a) As a believer, what decisions have you made without consulting the Lord?

Personal answers.

b) What were the results?

Personal answers.

Sometimes leaving God out of our decisions results in disappointment and discouragement. Other poor choices may have lifelong implications.

c) Has God still used this in your life?

Personal answers.

God often uses these situations to turn us back to Him and help us realize the folly of not including Him in decisions. But even when we have made serious mistakes, God still loves us and is able to work for our good in conforming us to His likeness.

5. If you are abiding, can you be out of God's will? Why or why not?

We *cannot* be out of God's will if we are abiding. We will be presenting what we think, what we say, and what we do to the Lord, and He promises to direct us. If we *ask* Him to guide us, we can be confident that He *will*.

6. What have you learned so far in this study that makes it easier to trust God to lead you?

Personal answers.

Hopefully your group members will be able to share how what they've learned so far has helped them seek the Lord and trust Him in all areas of their lives. The truths about our significance to God, His sovereignty and purpose, and the abiding and presenting provisions He has made for us to live godly lives should make it easier to trust Him to lead us.

7. a) What methods does God use to give us direction?

Circumstances—God can change the circumstances surrounding a decision. He may open doors to certain options and close others. He may bring new people into our lives. He may cause things to happen to us or to people around us to give us new or different leading. He occasionally interrupts a direction in which we are headed and gives us new opportunities. He sometimes uses the advice of godly people to verify what is scriptural or to help us see the situation or ourselves in a different light.

God gives us His mind and His desires—When we abide and seek His direction, He will guide our thoughts as we think about our circumstances or decisions. He will give us the desires of our hearts (place His desires in our hearts) and make us excited about and interested in what He wants us to do. If we are abiding and truly want God's will and if we present a decision to God and ask for His guidance, we can go ahead with what we think and feel is the best decision. We can move based on what we would really like to do, because we will have the mind of Christ on the decision.

Peace—He will give us peace or lack of peace. Sometimes the peace comes only after we have trusted God and made a move.

b) Can you give examples of knowing, possibly in hindsight, that God directed you? Did He use any of the methods you listed above?

Personal answers.

8. a) What decision(s) are you facing now or in the near future?

Personal answers.

b) Taking into consideration the methods listed above, has anything happened that might indicate leading from the Lord on these decisions?

Personal answers.

Try to help your group think through how God's methods of giving direction might apply to their personal situations.

9. God says He will place His desires on our hearts and minds, but what must we do first (Psalm 37:4–5)?

We must be soft, pliable, moldable—in other words, truly want His will, whatever it might be.

10. If you were to share the information presented in this chapter with a friend, what main points would you communicate?

a) God has a specific, personal will for each person. Both Jesus and Paul modeled this.

b) There are two areas of God's will. One is His general will—the instructions in Scripture that apply equally to all Christians. The other is His specific will that is unique to each individual and is revealed as he or she abides in the Lord.

c) God's will *primarily* involves our relationship with Him or with other people, not with things.

d) God gives us direction 1) through circumstances, 2) by giving us His mind and His desires, and 3) through peace or lack of it.

e) The most important question is not what God wants me to *do* or where He wants me to *go,* but *"Am I abiding and presenting? Do I honestly want God's control and leading in my life?"* If so, God promises to direct our steps.

11. From your journal page or highlighted text, what points—major or minor—were most significant to you and why?

Personal answers.

HOW SHOULD

I PRAY?

Primary Goal of Chapter 10

To encourage people to evaluate if their prayer life is in line with the instruction and modeling in Scripture. Nonbiblical prayer can result in discouragement, confusion, and a lack of confidence in the Lord.

Overview

Prayer, our two-way communication with God, is an extension of our abiding relationship with Him. In this chapter we will look at:

1. Why God does or does not answer prayer
2. What Jesus taught on prayer

1. Why does God answer some of our prayers and not others?
   - The primary reason for unanswered prayer is that we do not follow scriptural principles and Jesus' model of depending on the Father for everything. We can do nothing of eternal significance on our own, and everything—including prayer—must originate from God.
   - When we initiate prayer ourselves, quite often it is self-serving and comes from wrong motives (James 4:3). God will never answer prayer that leads us away from an abiding relationship with Him and from accomplishing His purpose of conforming us to the image of Jesus Christ.
   - The key to answered prayer is found in John 15:7, which we also looked at in the previous chapter about knowing God's will. *"If you abide in Me, and My words abide in you, ask whatever you wish, and it shall be done for you."* When we know what God says in

His Word, we will not pray for things He has not promised. When we abide in Him, He places in our hearts and minds the things we should pray. These are things He intends to answer for our good.

- Answered prayers are part of God's conforming process. As He demonstrates Himself to us, our ability to trust Him grows.

2. What did Jesus teach on prayer?

Jesus gave us a model for prayer in Matthew 6:9–13.

- The prayer is basically six commands: Five relate to spiritual needs, and one is for physical needs. The first three commands in the prayer will happen whether we pray or not. If we pray to be personally involved with God in these three areas, we will be changed. Our prayers in the rest of this model can, to some degree, change our circumstances.
- *Our Father who art in heaven*—He is our loving and caring Father, and we have a unique oneness with all other believers. He may be prompting others to pray the same things we are praying.
- *Hallowed be Thy name*—When we pray this way, it affects us. We will be changed as we recognize His sovereignty and holiness and present ourselves for His transformation.
- *Thy kingdom come*—When we pray for His kingdom to come, we're telling God that we are available if He wants to include us when He draws others to Himself. It's asking Him to make us aware of opportunities to share Jesus with others and give us His words to say. Seeing God work in the lives of others will profoundly affect our relationship with Him. We will be changed.
- *Thy will be done*—Praying for God's will in our lives requires that we accept even our painful situations as something God has allowed to conform us to the image of Christ. Even in hard times, we should approach the Lord with a desire to abide, an attitude of supplication, and dependency on His leading in all things. When we pray that His will be done in our lives, we will be transformed!
- *Give us this day our daily bread*—We need to ask the Father each day to meet our physical and material needs because in doing so, we remind ourselves that He is the one who provides for us. If we abide and present, God promises to meet our material needs, but we must trust His timing. If we look to material things for security, God may withhold extra blessings to get our attention.
- *Forgive us our sins*—As we abide in Christ, we ask Him to point out the areas in our lives that need to be purged. If we do not acknowledge our sin, recognize that it has already been paid for, and thank the Lord for forgiveness, then we do not *experience* the forgiveness that is ours through Christ's death on the cross.
- *Keep us from temptation*—We should pray, "Lord, I am desperately dependent on You to keep me abiding, to keep my old nature under Your control. Please keep me from sinning today." If we don't, we will continue to struggle with temptation.

Jesus also taught that we are to:
- *Pray for those who persecute us* (Matthew 5:43–45). He wants us to trust Him with all our relationships, even the difficult ones. When we abide, we can ask Him to let us see others through His eyes.
- *Pray for workers for His harvest* (Matthew 9:36–38). He is the one who gives new life, but He allows us to be a part of that by pointing people to Him.

- *Pray for nonbelievers when God prompts us.* He places people on our minds and hearts. The reason He does not instruct us to pray for the salvation of others is because we should not take the initiative concerning what God, the author of new life, will do in the lives of individual nonbelievers. He will prompt us to pray for those He will bring into His family.
- *Pray in Jesus' name.* This is to acknowledge that we are in total submission to Him.

The challenge for each of us is to align our prayer life with God's will and with Scripture. We need to pray daily that He will prompt us with what we should pray. An obedient, submissive, abiding relationship with Jesus is the key to effective, biblical prayer. *"Pray on every occasion,* as the Spirit leads" (Ephesians 6:18, TEV, emphasis added).

Points to Emphasize

We should follow Jesus' example of never taking the initiative in *any* area of life, and this includes prayer. We should ask God to lead and prompt us in what to pray for. Our instruction is in John 15:7—to abide in Him and have His words abide in us (to know Scripture). Because only God can give eternal life, we should ask Him to prompt us when to pray for individual nonbelievers. If we are listening to God for His prompting in all things, we will find ourselves fulfilling Paul's admonition to "pray without ceasing."

Possible Issues

For some, this chapter will be exciting and freeing. Others may struggle with having their prayer habits challenged. If this happens to some in your group, encourage them to examine if the way they pray has been based on scriptural principles or if it's just what they have been taught or modeled. All the doctrines we have studied concerning our relationship of dependency on God should also be the basis for how we pray.

Please Note: There is so much Scripture about prayer that this chapter is limited to only what Jesus taught. Even though there is much more teaching on prayer, a major theme of all Scripture is our dependency on and trust in God's leading, and this has to include prayer.

Discussion Questions and Possible Answers

The questions in this chapter will help us realize that prayer is just another manifestation of our abiding, presenting, and dependent relationship with the Lord. We should not take the initiative in prayer any more than we should in other areas of our walk with God. This chapter may challenge some of the things your group members may have believed about prayer. Encourage them to stay focused on the content of the chapter and, if they struggle with some of it, to study it on their own and in light of everything else we have learned about our relationship with God.

Question 1a helps us see why our prayers sometimes go unanswered. We pay attention to how God prompts us in our prayer with Question 2a, while 3 helps us realize what kinds of things we're praying for—spiritual or physical. Please be extra sensitive when you get to Questions 6 and 7. These are very personal, and I recommend you pass over them unless someone wants to share their answers with the group.

Encourage your group members to talk openly about how their understanding of prayer has changed and how that understanding relates to the entire study.

1. a) Why does God not answer some of our prayers the way we want Him to?

   Instead of asking God to prompt us with what to pray, we initiate prayer on our own. Often our prayers are self-serving and come from wrong motives (James 4:3). We pray for things that we believe will make us happy and comfortable. We may pray for relief from situations that God has allowed or brought about to conform us or to get our attention. Sometimes we do not know Scripture well enough and pray for things God has not promised. Frequently we ask things of God that, for our good, He will not answer.

   b) What things have you not received that you prayed for, and can you now see the reason why?

   Personal answers.

   Most of us can look back at things we prayed for that we now realize would not have been good for us. Encourage your group to share these experiences.

2. a) Explain how God "prompts" us in our prayers.

   If we are abiding and asking for God's mind, He simply guides our thoughts and actions. Our responsibility is to present ourselves for His leading and prompting. If we seriously ask God to guide our thoughts and prompt us in what to pray, we can confidently pray the things that come into our minds, knowing He has placed them there.

   b) Have you ever felt God prompting you or seen in hindsight that He did? Be specific.

   Personal answers.

3. Five of the six requests in the Lord's Prayer are for spiritual needs and one is for physical or material needs.

   a) List the kinds of things you pray for individually and in groups. Are the requests mostly for spiritual or for physical and material needs?

   Personal answers.

   We frequently pray for health, relationships, jobs, and finances. Most of us will realize that our prayers, and the prayers of other people, center much more on our physical and material needs or for God to change our circumstances than on our spiritual needs. It is not wrong to pray for material things, but the question is, are these prayers a result of God's leading?

   b) What are some spiritual needs (attitudes, emotions, actions—things that affect your relationship with God and others) that you could pray about in your own life?

Personal answers.

We should pray more for Him to change our attitudes and control our emotions, for us to be in His will, for us to be obedient to Him, and for us to get to know Him and allow Him to conform us to His likeness. You may get some good examples from your group.

4. The first three requests of the Lord's Prayer will happen whether we pray them or not. If we pray them, we will be changed. In your own words, paraphrase how you personally could pray for these things.

Following are some things that might be included under each phrase:

Hallowed be Thy name—God is continually praised by the angels and hosts of heaven. We can pray that *today* all our thoughts, all our words, and all the things we do will be prompted by Him and will be a natural response because we are abiding. We can ask Him to prompt us when we should thank and honor Him, when we should ask for His direction, or when we should ask Him for the Christlike response to a person or situation. Our prayers in this area would be to tell the Lord that we are desperately dependent on Him and that our desire is to abide. We can ask Him to keep us abiding, because on our own we will not. If we are abiding, He will be honored in how we live.

Thy kingdom come—God is the one who gives new life and brings people into His kingdom. We must recognize that any sin of omission on our part will not prevent God from blessing other people and giving them new life. If God wants us involved in this area so that we will see Him at work in other people's lives, our sin of omission will be detrimental to us. We will miss experiences He wants us to have so that we grow and trust Him more. Our prayers should recognize that He may want us to be involved as He brings people into the kingdom or to a deeper relationship with Jesus Christ. It would be a wonderful way to see Him demonstrate Himself, and it would grow our relationship with Him. We should pray that we will be very sensitive to people He brings into our lives and that, when He prompts us, we will be ready to give a reason for the faith that is within us (1 Peter 3:15).

Thy will be done—God's will *will* be done, and we cannot help it or stop it. Our first concern is to have a totally submissive heart, to trust Him fully, to recognize that He is in control, loves us, and knows what is best. We should also pray that we will be in such an abiding relationship that He will use us as instruments in anything He wants to do with other people. We will automatically be in the places He wants us to be and do the things He wants us to do. Most important, we want to become the person He wants us to be, in the process of being conformed to His image.

5. "Give us this day our daily bread."

a) What material and physical needs are you praying for?

Personal answers.

b) Which are the hardest to wait for and trust Him with day by day?

Personal answers.

6. "And forgive us our debts [sins] . . ."

   a) Do you still feel guilt and lack of forgiveness for past sins from which you have turned away? (Ask God to give you assurance that you are forgiven, because Christ died for those sins.)

   Very personal answers.

   Tell your group you will skip over these two questions unless someone would like to share their struggles and ask for prayer support. Give enough time for someone to respond, then move on. If anyone chooses to respond, this could be a very significant time for your group.

   b) Is there still sin for which you have never truly repented (specifically admitted to God with an honest desire to turn from it)?

   Very personal answers.

7. "And do not lead us into temptation . . ."

   List areas in which you sometimes experience unexpected temptation.

   Personal answers.

   The list will be varied. Some possible answers:
   - Lust and sexual sin
   - Unhealthy relationships
   - Addictive substances
   - Finances (worrying, planning, manipulating)
   - Pride
   - Anger
   - Revenge
   - Defying authority
   - Condemning other people/gossiping

8. a) Why are we not instructed, or modeled, to pray for the salvation of individual non-Christians?

   God is the only one who gives life. He is the only one who can bring people into His family. We are saved through faith, not of ourselves; it is a gift from God (Ephesians 2:8–9). This truth is repeated in many other passages of Scripture. Only God knows whom He will bring to Himself. Consequently, if we pray for the lost on our own initiative, many of our prayers will go unanswered.

The key lesson God wants to teach us is that we have to trust His wisdom in this extremely significant and emotional area of our lives. Hopefully your group will understand that biblical prayer is letting God prompt us to pray the things that He intends to answer.

b) When should we pray for the salvation of individual nonbelievers?

The first thing we have to determine is whether we are abiding. If we are, *we should pray for a nonbeliever when God prompts us*—when He places people on our minds and hearts and gives us a burden for them. We can then pray for them with confidence, knowing God is at work in their lives and, in His timing, He will bring them to Himself.

9. John 15:7 says: *"If you abide in Me, and My words abide in you, ask whatever you wish, and it shall be done for you."*

a) How can God make this promise?

God can unconditionally promise answered prayers when we are abiding because He will prompt us to pray for the things He wants to share with us and do for us. John 15:7 was used in the previous chapter to show that both knowing Scripture and abiding in Christ are essential to know God's will. In this question, the verse is used again to show that only when we meet these two conditions can God promise to answer all our prayers. It is very important that your group understands these two conditions.

b) Express in your own words what these two conditions mean to you.

Personal answers.

One condition is that His words abide in us—that we know the guidelines of Scripture so we will not be praying for something He has never promised. The second condition is that we abide in Him—that we are desperately dependent on Him for everything: our thoughts, our attitudes, our responses, and even what we pray.

10. Has your understanding of prayer changed throughout this study? If so, how?

Personal answers.

Encourage your group to talk openly about how their understanding of prayer has changed and how their understanding relates to the entire study.

Below are some of the principles we have studied that might affect prayer. You could use these as guides if you want to stimulate more discussion. *Your group will not, and need not, include all of these.*

Do I matter to God?—When we know that God loves us and is concerned with our needs, we are more willing to present them and believe that He hears us.

Is God really in control?—When we understand that He is totally sovereign, in complete control, and able to answer our prayers, we will pray with more confidence that He can do something about our situation. We will also make fewer "demands" of what He should or should not do. We will let God be God and trust Him.

Does God have a purpose for my life?—Our prayers will change as we get a better understanding of His purpose for us—that we are to get to know Him and that He wants to conform us into the image of Jesus Christ, or give us His nature. We know that the fruit of the Spirit is what is significant, even more than *where* we are, *what* we do, and what we *have*.

How does God really see me?—As we begin to recognize our limitations and our desperate dependence on God, we will include Him in more things because we realize we can deceive ourselves.

What does it mean to abide?—The two key things regarding the Vine are: 1) apart from Him we can do nothing, and 2) the fruit produced is the fruit of the *Spirit*. "Apart from Me" includes praying, and we need to ask God to prompt us with what to pray. We should concentrate more on praying that God will produce the fruit of the Spirit in our lives rather than asking Him to give us things or change our circumstances.

What is my part and what is God's part?—We should learn to present all aspects of our lives to God, recognizing that *He* is the one who will do the "unconforming" and the transforming in our lives. We will stop asking God to help *us* change and ask Him to do the changing in us. We should ask God to reveal to us where we are conformed to this world and what we should present.

How should I respond to difficult circumstances?—We should ask God to help us identify not only the circumstances and emotions we struggle with, but also the attitudes that make us react in the ways we do. We should present the things we are anxious about to the Lord and trust Him to give us the peace He promises.

How can I know God's will for my life?—We should concentrate on our desire to abide with Him and be in submission to Him. Then we can pray with confidence for Him to direct our steps, to open and close doors, to guide our thoughts and our desires, and to give us peace.

11. If you were to share the information presented in this chapter with a friend, what main points would you communicate?

    a) The first three requests of the Lord's Prayer will happen whether we pray them or not. If we do pray in these areas, *we* will be changed.

    b) We need to pray the second three requests to receive the *fullness* of God's blessing. To get our attention and cause us to turn to Him, He may even withhold some things He would otherwise like to give us.

    c) Jesus' temptation in the wilderness was to not wait for the Father's timing, but to take control of the situation and meet His own needs.

d) Godly prayer is initiated by God.

e) Scripture does not instruct us or model for us to pray for the salvation of individual non-believers. We should pray for people's salvation when God prompts us.

12. From your journal page or highlighted text, what points—major or minor—were most significant to you and why?

Personal answers.

HOW DO I KNOW IF MY FAITH IS GROWING?

Primary Goal of Chapter 11

To help us see how important our faith is to God and how a growing faith is developed.

Overview

As mentioned in the first chapter, we are maturing as believers if, instead of trying to solve or handle things on our own, we are trusting the Lord more quickly and with more and bigger things. This kind of maturity comes as our faith reservoir is enlarged. In this chapter we look at:

1. How God increases our faith and our responsibility in the process
2. The "giants" we may face in this faith-building process and the weapons we should use

1. How God increases our faith and our responsibility in the process
   - Scripture tells us that without faith it is impossible to please God, yet it also tells us that God has to give us faith—both for salvation and to live our daily lives.
   - As believers, *we must start the process of God giving us faith*. When we face a problem, rather than focusing on the struggle and trying to solve it by ourselves, we must recognize our dependence on God and present the circumstance, emotion, or attitude.
   - God then increases our faith by demonstrating Himself to us when we present. He meets

our need, gives us His perspective, or changes our hearts and minds. Each time we see God's faithfulness to us, it is easier to trust Him in the next situation.

- David is an example of this faith building. Because God had protected him from danger over and over again in the past, he knew God would take care of Goliath. His faith was based on evidence of God's past faithfulness.

2. The "giants" we may face in this faith-building process and the weapons we should use
   - Just as Goliath wanted David to fight with him alone, Satan wants us to fight our old sin nature on our own. When we are abiding and presenting, we have God Himself to fight for us. He replaces our sin nature with His own character.
   - Looking to money and material possessions for our security and significance can be a "giant." This can only be overcome by our growing confidence that God is able to take care of us and has promised to meet our needs.
   - Many other cultural "giants" taunt us: sexual sin, addictions, bad relationships, fear, and the humanistic view of man (that we are born good but learn to be bad). The trend toward tolerance goes against God's Word that truth is absolute, that there is right and wrong. We are the minority in this world. Only God went with David to meet Goliath, and God is always with us, overcoming these temptations by giving us His character.
   - Just as David faced persecution for trusting God with Goliath, we may be ridiculed by Christians who do not understand our desire to trust the Lord in all situations.
   - In the same way that David could not use Saul's armor, we cannot fight the giants of this world with the weapons of this world: our intelligence, experience, power, money, or better methods. Although, like David, we will be involved in the battle, we must choose to let God fight the giants for us, always recognizing that He is the one who gives us the victory, accomplishes any ministry, and transforms us into His image.

Finally, we see that God commends the Bible's faith heroes not for their accomplishments, but for their faith. *Building faith is a process.* The more we present and God demonstrates Himself to us, the easier the process becomes. We come to know that He is in control of everything, that He loves us unconditionally, and that we are desperately dependent on Him and cannot become godly on our own. We watch Him change our attitudes, our emotions, and sometimes our circumstances. Our reservoir of faith is enlarged, and it becomes easier to trust Him more quickly and for more and bigger things.

Points to Emphasize

Faith—our growing trust in God in more and bigger circumstances—is evidence of our maturing. Faith increases in our Christian walk like this: We present something to the Lord, He acts (demonstrates Himself) on our behalf, and our faith in Him grows. But we have to take the first step by presenting.

Possible Issues

There should not be any issues brought up in this chapter.

Discussion Questions and Possible Answers

The questions in this chapter will help your group members clarify their understanding of faith and understand the goal of spiritual growth: to develop deeper levels of trust and dependence on God. Several questions should be an encouragement as people look at their growth, while also being honest about where they are right now.

Because this is the final chapter, *be sure to spend time on Question 11.* You may even want to try to schedule an extra session or a social time to cover this. Encourage your group to share freely and rejoice in a more intimate, biblical relationship with the Lord.

1. a) What has been your understanding of faith in the past?

    Personal answers.

    Some people believe it is our responsibility to develop and exercise faith out of our own human abilities. Others have believed that if you have enough faith, it is a means of getting God to respond in the way you want. They think that God is not responding to our needs or prayers because we don't have enough faith. Others believe that you must get a number of people together who have strong faith to ensure that God answers their prayers. Still others have only a vague idea of what faith is.

    b) Has your perspective changed after reading this chapter? If so, how?

    Personal answers.

    Faith is a rational decision on our part because we have experienced God's faithfulness in the past, and we have confidence that we can trust Him in the present or the future.

2. Explain the process of how God gives us faith.

    (This is a "head knowledge" question so that your group will thoroughly understand the process.)

    God gave us a measure of faith when He redeemed us. The process for this faith to grow must now start with us. We have the responsibility to present ourselves to God. When we present something and submit to His will in the matter (Romans 12:1), He then acts on our behalf. We see God's demonstration of faithfulness to us, that He is loving, sovereign, and in control of everything. We see Him change our attitudes and our emotions and, in some cases, our circumstances (Romans 12:2—He "unconforms" us and transforms us). As a result, our faith in Him is increased (Romans 12:3—God gives us faith). This starts stretching our "reservoir of faith," our history of experiencing God's faithfulness to us. The next time we face a decision or difficult situation, it is easier to trust Him. We are then able to do it more quickly and in larger situations, which is evidence of spiritual maturing.

3. List specific examples of how God has given you more faith (increased your ability to trust Him) by:

a) answering prayer

b) changing circumstances

c) changing you

Personal answers.

4. What circumstances, emotions, or attitudes were you not able to trust God with in the past that you're now able to?

Personal answers.

5. What was most significant to you in the account of David and Goliath?

Personal answers.

6. a) List the "giants" in your life right now.

Personal answers.

Some of the giants people struggle with are money, pride, desire for status or power, and pressure to measure up to the world's standard of success. Other giants are singleness or problems in marriage or with children. To some a need to be loved, their own self-worth (which is a comparison of themselves with others), or a need for security are giants. Giants for some people are peer pressures in the areas of drugs or alcohol, lust in their thought life, or pressures to conform to the world in sexual temptation and behavior. Many people are actually addicted to things like work, exercise, television, video games, the Internet, or shopping. The list can go on and on. Your group will probably come up with many more.

Remember that money, education, and other good things are not necessarily giants in themselves. They become detrimental when they are the focus of our lives to gain significance, security, or purpose.

b) What were giants in your past?

Personal answers.

c) Why are these no longer giants for you?

Personal answers.

Most likely they have more confidence that God is in control of all things, that He is good, and that He loves them unconditionally. They may have begun to present more circumstances, emotions, and attitudes to God and have seen Him change them. This has given them a new focus, perspective, and stability.

7. What changes have you seen in your attitudes and lifestyle as you have matured in Christ?

   Personal answers.

   Most people who are maturing in Christ can see changes in their habits, lifestyle, thought life, attitudes, and ability to trust God. You might ask your group if they think these are changes brought about by God or if they have modified their behavior to impress people out of pressure from the Christian community.

8. Jesus sent out the disciples to minister without material provisions. He did this so they would have to trust God, but He sent them in twos so they could encourage each other. Write down times when:

   a) other people have encouraged you to trust God

   b) you have seen God meet your material needs when you were not sure how it would happen

   Personal answers.

9. If you were to share the information presented in this chapter with a friend, what main points would you communicate?

   a) We measure our Christian maturity by how much faith *God* has given us.

   b) God gives us faith when we present things and see Him demonstrate Himself.

   c) How much we *trust* God and then act in obedience—not what we appear to accomplish—is important.

   d) A growing faith in God is what gives us the ability to turn over even more control of our lives to Him.

10. From your journal page or highlighted text, what points—major or minor—were most significant to you and why?

    Personal answers.

11. What has God taught you from this entire study that has changed your relationship with Him?

    Personal answers.

    Have a great time rejoicing in the faithfulness of God!

A Final Word

My wife, Betty, and I pray that as you and your group journeyed through *Discovery* that you grew in your understanding of God, what He wants to do in your lives, and how that is accomplished. We have a sovereign God who is in complete control, and because He loves us, we can trust Him to know what is best for us. How freeing it is to know that we do not have to just *act* like Jesus. He wants to conform us into His image—inside and out—by sharing His character with us. He will transform us as we abide and present everything to Him. Even though we are buffeted on all sides by our "do-it-yourself" world, we pray that you and your group have made this important realization: If Jesus Himself did not take any initiative but only did what the Father instructed Him, then we should live the same way. We hope that the words "desperately dependent" will become very real to you as you depend on Him for all transformation and direction.

Because of the amount of Scripture and content in *Discovery,* most people tell us they need to go back through the study again. We suggest that you encourage your group to do this sometime in the near future. An even better idea is that they lead others through it. You have probably seen the value of facilitating a group.

May your walk with the Lord become increasingly intimate, dependent, trusting, and comfortable. If I can be of any assistance to you, please feel free to contact me.

WILL WYATT
wyatt@dfocus.org

WANTED

COLLEGE AND CAREER-AGE YOUNG ADULTS

FOR 10 WEEKS OF INTENSE DISCIPLESHIP

Discipleship Focus is a 10-week summer discipleship program for college and career-age young adults at Silver Dollar City in Branson, Missouri, and Dollywood in Pigeon Forge, Tennessee.

In partnership with Young Life, *Discovery* author and his wife, Betty, started this program in 1977.

The Discipleship Focus program includes:
- Indepth biblical study using *Discovery*
- Small-group interaction and one-on-one mentoring with caring staff
- Employment at an exciting theme park
- Friendship with peers from across the country
- The opportunity to love and serve others living in the community and at work

To order other DISCOVERY materials . . .

Discovery: God's Answers to Our Deepest Questions
The 11-chapter Bible study designed to answer a Christian's basic questions about God and the kind of relationship He wants with us.

Discovery Leader's Guide
Contains all the information you need to facilitate a *Discovery* discussion group.

Here I Am: Worship songs of the Discovery Bible Study
With songs composed and recorded by Scott Lisea, a Young Life regional director in California, *Here I Am* can be used with the *Discovery* Bible study or enjoyed on its own. Scott was compelled to write this worship music after being profoundly influenced by *Discovery*.

Set of 10 CDs of Will Wyatt's teaching on *Discovery*
These were recorded at Discipleship Focus, the summer program the Wyatts lead at Silver Dollar City in Branson, Missouri. Though the teaching is very similar to the book, the CDs do not follow the book exactly. Available only from Discipleship Focus.